Hope in Front of Me

DANNY GOKEY

WITH BEN STROUP

Find Purpose in Your Darkest Moments

Hope in Front of Me

NavPress is the publishing ministry of The Navigators, an international Christian organization and leader in personal spiritual development. NavPress is committed to helping people grow spiritually and enjoy lives of meaning and hope through personal and group resources that are biblically rooted, culturally relevant, and highly practical.

For a free catalog go to www.NavPress.com or call 1.800.366.7788 in the United States or 1.800.839.4769 in Canada.

ISBN-13: 978-1-61291-475-6 (hardback)
ISBN-13: 978-1-61291-613-2 (paperback)

Cover design by Faceout Studio, Charles Brock
Cover photo by Kristin Barlowe

Some of the anecdotal illustrations in this book are true to life and are included with the permission of the persons involved. All other illustrations are composites of real situations, and any resemblance to people living or dead is coincidental. Names have been changed to protect the people involved.

Cataloging-in-Publication Data is available.

Printed in the United States of America

1 2 3 4 5 6 7 8 / 18 17 16 15 14 13

This book is dedicated to everyone who knows they have more deep down inside of them but are broken, disappointed, and wounded. I hope that through my story you find encouragement, greater resolve, and the inner fight to push forward.

Contents

Foreword

Every person on this planet has a calling on their life. There is something so special and unique for every person, something that defines them. The world has been built by the dreams and aspirations of ordinary people. Oftentimes, people look upon the success of others and view it as an exclusive privilege open to just a select few. The truth is, not only is it possible to do what you love and thrive but it is your God-given calling.

For as long as I have known Danny Gokey, he has been a man of integrity who understands his identity. He possesses great character and a powerful drive to succeed. He knows what he is passionate about, and he is unafraid to pursue his dreams no matter how hard or demanding that may be. Danny does not compromise his values when the world tries to change him. He is constantly focused on God's calling, and this is what drives his thoughts and actions.

Everybody has something great that they were destined to do with their life. To be truly satisfying, this cause must involve serving others. Many times, people gain all the things they dream of but still feel empty and unfulfilled. This is because if our dreams do not involve serving others, we will never feel complete. An amazing joy is released when helping someone; it is ingrained into our altruistic nature as human beings. To take advantage of our God-given calling, we must understand what we are passionate about and learn how to use that passion outwardly in service of others.

When people look back on Danny's life, they will see a legacy of compassion and generosity. Through his charity, Sophia's Heart, Danny has helped so many people get back on their feet and rebuild their lives. He has worked tirelessly to help the less fortunate, providing them with temporary housing, job training, life skills, and food. Danny has been running this organization for only a short time, but the impact it has had on his community is undeniable, and he will reach even more people in the future. He has found a purpose that is bigger than himself—something that gives him a whole new outlook on life. This is the mentality of serving. When you live with a servant's mind-set, you will constantly be searching for new ways to help and thinking of more efficient ways to do so. When you live with outstretched arms, you will always find greater opportunities and more abundant resources.

Life is a wonderful mystery that takes many unexpected turns. Even the greatest saint will have times of heartache and pain. In these trying times, pain can either break us down or build us up. Life is what we make it; it is all about perspective. We can choose to see only heartache and misery, or we can be aware that such things are necessary parts of life, but they don't have to control us. Without sorrow, happiness would have no meaning. Without loss, we would not understand what it means to gain something. This doesn't mean we are supposed to be carefree and oblivious all of the time. It is true that there will be difficult situations, but how we face these difficult times, learn their lessons, and move on with greater wisdom is what defines us. Our quality of life is heavily influenced by our attitude; every day we make a decision to either embrace joy or give in to sadness. The choice is up to us.

When I think of Danny, I see a man of great compassion and

amazing courage. When he was met with unbelievable tragedy, he continued to persevere. His faith guided him through the darkness and opened up the unlimited possibilities of his future. By trusting in God, Danny found healing and a renewed purpose. It is so easy to give up and wallow in self-pity, but it takes a great deal of courage to move forward and build life anew in the face of tragedy. Life will not always work out the way we plan, and sometimes it feels impossible to let go of the pain. There is total comfort in knowing that God is guiding us every step of the way and is preparing a future of unlimited possibilities and abundant blessing.

Danny is a perfect example of how to succeed by living a life of faith, integrity, and determination. God has blessed him with amazing talent, and he embraces that talent with passion and responsibility. He understands the value of hard work and determination and that no matter how difficult life may be, we must always fight for what we believe in. Danny is guided by his faith; he trusts that God has a plan for his life and that no matter what challenges he may face, there is always hope for a brighter day. He understands the importance of staying true to himself. He never forsakes his values, and he always treats others with respect. He has found the one thing he was called to do, and he uses his talents for the good of the world.

When you do what you love, you will always find renewed inspiration. The only calling that matters is to be the solution to the world's problems and constantly search for ways to serve others. That is how you find true happiness and live a complete, fulfilled life. The answer is right in front of you, if you would only embrace it.

—Pastor Matthew Barnett,
cofounder, The Dream Center

Acknowledgments

Thankful doesn't begin to describe my appreciation for the people and circumstances over the course of my life that have been a part of writing my story and realizing my hopes and dreams.

God, thank You for taking my brokenness and making something beautiful out of it.

To my beautiful wife, Leyicet, you have always encouraged me. You and my son, Daniel, were the chapter in my book I could not see when my world fell apart.

To my mom, dad, brother, and sisters, we've been through so much and have endured many painful moments together, but our bonds are stronger than ever and our best is yet to come.

To Sophia's family, thank you for taking me in and loving me like your own.

To all my mentors and spiritual leaders who believed in me and helped me to become who I am today, thank you for investing in me.

To Penny, thank you for always pushing me to be my best me and for your help making this book what it needed to be. You are a godsend.

To Rebekah Guzman and the NavPress team, thank you for

catching the vision for this project and your patience in allowing me to take the time I needed to perfect and finish the book. I truly appreciate the belief and support you've shown for Sophia's Heart.

To Ben Stroup, thank you for capturing my random stories, thoughts, and ideas and bringing them to life on the page. I know it was a huge effort, and I appreciate all of your efforts.

To the staff and volunteers at Sophia's Heart, the passion you all possess to see broken lives restored invigorates me. And to the families in our program at Sophia's Heart past and present, you guys inspire me. I see God in you.

Introduction

Hope means nothing—unless it's all you have. That's what makes hope dangerous, unpredictable, and life changing. It can make us believe the impossible is possible, shielding the mind and guarding the heart from the difficulty right in front us. Without hope, our dreams seem out of reach, unlikely, and impossible.

From preachers to peddlers, everyone seems to be selling some type of hope, and we are all ready to buy. We look for hope in others. We look for hope in the achievement of things like power, position, and prestige. But those who find true hope know it is found only when we look through the eyes of our hearts.

Hope is the thread that runs through the fabric of our lives. We have all hoped for something. We celebrate when our hope connects us to something better. We are devastated when what we had hoped for doesn't come to be in the time or way we expected. We hope because it feels as natural as breathing.

No matter how outrageous or impossible, we can't let go of hope. If we do, we give up. And giving up is not a path to a complete, satisfying, and fulfilling life.

When we no longer have hope, a part of us dies. Our world feels small, limited, and scary. Without hope, we lose clarity, confidence, and cadence. Hope is where we find reason to live and to make our way in the world.

We are never more alive than when we are filled with hope for what could be. We must have hope. It may be the only real thing that exists.

Your Story Isn't Finished

Wherever you are, whatever you've been through, however dark and dangerous your life is, hope is the magic you've been missing. It may not be tangible. You may not be able to show it to someone else. But it is what you hold on to — your deed of ownership, if you will — until what you hope for comes to be.

Hope means everything. It will move you forward with a sense of possibility and confidence that good things are within reach. I'm excited about what's next for you, and I can't wait to read or hear about your story one day.

Many people may recognize me from *American Idol*, but my story begins long before I appeared on the show and continues on in ways I never could've anticipated. This book is my story, much of which you've likely never read online or heard in an interview. My dreams began to form as a child. My purpose is found in the relationships that mean the most to me. My destiny was born out of my darkest moments. Throughout all of my experiences, one thing remained constant: hope.

American Idol changed my life but not in the way you might expect. For me, fame has never been something I wanted. Fame comes and goes. My desire has always been to lead a life of significance. I want to leave my mark on the people who have been lost, forgotten, and counted out. I was found in the crowd, but I am no more deserving than anyone else to know that someone cares.

When my first wife, Sophia, died, I wanted her love for children and families to live on. That's why I started Sophia's Heart. I wanted to make sure those who never were able to know Sophia would be able to know her through the love poured out for those who live tucked away in the margins of society. Through Sophia's Heart, we are helping people articulate their dreams and then giving them the tools to dramatically impact their sense of hope for the future.

I bet I'm a lot like you: a person full of struggles and pain as well as hopes and dreams. The hope that is before me is the same hope before you. My prayer is that in the midst of telling you my story, you will find meaning for your own story.

The things you experience today are preparing you for the next step in your journey. Your story isn't complete, so don't write yourself off. Your story is bigger than you can imagine.

Life is too short, the stakes are too high, and the opportunity to make a difference too significant to live without hope.

No matter what decisions you have made, you are not limited by your past.

No matter what others say, you are not limited by what others see.

No matter what your situation, you are not limited by your present circumstance.

Hope is yours for the taking. It is available to you right where you are, whether you are at the pinnacle of success or the depths of failure. Hope is right in front of you. There is no catch. You just have to choose to believe—in hope and in yourself.

Chapter 1

Living Through the Eyes of My Heart

Your heart is your real set of eyes.

Faith does not preclude us from being broken. Instead, faith gives us the strength to hold on to hope when everything comes crashing down. This is what I believe.

Sophia and I believed for a miracle, but the miracle hadn't come. We were worn out and tired. We were discouraged. We needed to see the events take a different turn. There had to be a sign somewhere that better days were ahead of us.

I was sixteen the first time I laid eyes on Sophia. At that time, I was working at a sub shop, going to school, and just living life. I noticed that many of the people around me were in some type of relationship. I wanted a girlfriend. I wanted to know what it felt like to have a special relationship with another person.

I believe that every person was designed to love and be loved. This is what it means to be truly human, truly alive, and truly purposeful in our going and doing. To love and be loved is the greatest privilege we have in this life.

One night I was feeling particularly hopeless at the possibility of finding someone to share my life with. I was sitting in my car, thinking about my slim prospects, and I said a quick prayer to vent my frustration. I figured at this point, all help was welcome.

I turned on the radio, only to hear the song "You Must Have Been an Angel," by Bob Carlisle. It spoke to me.

Have you ever listened to a song and felt it resonate in your heart, like it meant something specific in that very moment? That's what it was like for me. It wasn't long after that I noticed her for the first time, and I remembered the prayer and the song. I took it as confirmation that this girl was special.

Her name was Sophia. We met at church at an end-of-summer party. The date—August 10, 1997—is etched in my memory.

We spent the next two years building a relationship—over the phone. Yes, that's right. It sounds out of date, I know. But Sophia's parents were very strict. I suspect having daughters can do that to a father. Her parents' Spanish heritage also influenced their expectations, as it is very different from American culture.

Really, I didn't care: We were in love—at least as best as we understood it at the time. We followed her parents' rules even though we didn't agree with them. We both respected her parents and knew that if we didn't follow their rules, we wouldn't have a chance of spending any time together.

Because all we had were phone calls, our conversations were amazing. I looked forward to them all week. I would come home and wait for Sophia to call. Sometimes I had to wait my turn to use our home phone because our family was large. It was excruciating at times. I just wanted whoever was on the phone to hang up so it would be my turn. It was always worth the wait though.

When Sophia turned eighteen, she was finally allowed to go on dates, except her sister had to go with us. There is nothing like being eighteen years old—old enough to vote, serve your country in war, and be legally responsible for yourself—and still needing a chaperone for a date with your girlfriend. It seemed old-fashioned, but I wanted to spend time with Sophia more than I cared about the rules of engagement.

Anytime I went over to Sophia's house, we had to sit in the living room. We couldn't venture to other parts of the house. We complied, though, because we wanted to keep the trust of her parents. It was a little bit of a shock at times, given the contrast with how things were at my house. It wasn't that my parents didn't care or have any rules; Sophia's parents just had more rules than pretty much anyone I knew. But I was completely comfortable going at the slow pace and sticking with the boundaries they set because I wanted to be with her. And she had my heart completely.

Sophia was really spunky. I guess it would be fair to say she was a fireball. She packed a lot of punch and had a quick wit. We could talk for hours, and I could tell her things I hadn't told anyone else. Sophia also loved kids. She worked with the kids at church, and there was rarely a time when I didn't see a child on her hip. She was everything I had hoped for when I heard Bob Carlisle sing.

The Dating Game

Sophia and I fell for each other pretty quickly and dated for several years. But as every lovestruck teenager knows, dating has its ups and downs. When you're young, you can be impulsive and hurtful without even trying. We fell into that category at times. As a result, we broke up and got back together more times than I care to count. In spite of that, we always had a connection that didn't fade, even when we did break up. At the end of the day, I knew she was the one for me, but anyone who has been in a serious relationship knows it is easy to lose yourself in the intense emotions you feel for one another. That's what happened to me.

Sophia and I continued to spend a lot of time together, and things became serious. I had the intention of marrying her, but I started recognizing the highs and lows in our relationship. I valued Sophia's opinion and respected her relationship with God, perhaps more than I did my own. When things were good between Sophia and me, everything was right with the world and with God. But when we hit a rough patch, my world turned upside down and I started to question myself. *Was I valuable? Was I attractive enough?* I recognized how dependent I was on Sophia, and I knew that wasn't right. I knew I needed some time away to be sure of who I was without Sophia.

We ended up breaking up for about a year. It wasn't an easy choice. We talked about it and decided that if we set our love free and came back to each other, it must be a match made in heaven. If not, we'd have saved ourselves from marrying the wrong person. I asked Sophia to promise me she would wait for me, and she said she would.

But just a few days after we broke up, Sophia was hanging out with another guy from the worship team at our church—the same team I was on—and I could do nothing but watch. All of our friends knew that Sophia and I dated for five years, and no one said anything about her hanging out with this other guy. I felt like it was blatantly in my face. I remember them leaving church together, just the two of them, and getting into his car right in front of me. It devastated me. I couldn't believe it. I went out to my car and cried my eyes out. In that moment, through the hurt I was feeling, I promised myself I wasn't going to rely on someone else to build me up and that I wouldn't run to another person to find out who I was.

When I was younger, my sisters always told me I was ugly. I know they didn't mean anything by it; it was just typical sibling stuff. But I was so impressionable. I looked up to them, and what they said affected me. I always heard them talk about boys and how cute they were, but they told me I was ugly, so I just assumed I was. It wasn't until my twenties that I realized girls like guys for who they are and not necessarily how good-looking they are, although I'm sure looks help. Reflecting back on that, I realize that what my sisters said to me shaped my view of who I was, as do many things when we're young.

Gradually, I began to see things differently. I started to let all the junk go, including the lies I believed about myself. I spent a lot of time praying and asking God to wash all the negative stuff out of me. And He did. I came to a place where I recognized who I was again and could be confident in that. Little did I know this setback in my relationship with Sophia was what I needed to bring me to a better place and ultimately bring us closer together in the end, though you never feel that way in the moment when your emotions are raw.

It took me six months just to get comfortable with the idea of not being with Sophia. She continued to date the same guy. I eventually dated other girls, but for me, nothing felt right. I couldn't talk to other girls the way I could to Sophia. There was just something off. I took that as a confirmation that Sophia was the one I was supposed to be with. I was hoping that dream would come true.

The good news is we *did* get back together. God made it clear to both of us that's what He wanted. No voice was spoken from heaven, no clouds parted, no doves came out of the sky. There is just something deep within that knows when you meet the other half of your soul. It is a connection that can be explained and understood only by the two halves intended to make a whole.

We were both twenty-three when we decided to get back together —this time for good. No more interruptions. No more bumps in the road. It was time to follow our hearts fully and put all other roads—other options, relationally speaking—behind us. This was for real—and forever.

It was destiny that we met. I am sure of it. So much of who I am and my own story is wrapped up in Sophia.

A Second Set of Eyes

The road to our destiny comes with a lot of on-ramps and off-ramps. It's easy to get distracted. Sometimes those distractions will take us off course, away from the destiny planted in our hearts. Even when we get off course, we have opportunities to get back on track, but there's no telling what people and experiences we may have missed during our detours. It's important to stay the course and commit wholeheartedly to following the dreams in your heart. The destiny given to you specifically is like a calibrated compass that will guide you along your journey through life. There are so many people and situations that can steer us in a variety of ways for a number of reasons. You can calculate your life away. In the end, you have to focus on the direction your heart is leading as you move forward into your future.

Your heart is a second set of eyes to help you see the things of this world. If your heart has become evil through seeds of anger and hate, you will interpret life and every person's actions through those negative eyes. A person might come shake your hand and compliment you, and your heart might analyze what they have done as having some kind of hidden motive or agenda. You might spend countless hours wondering why he or she is out to get you. On the other hand, if you have a pure heart, you accept the compliment and are touched by the person's kindness. All things are possible when we see life and people through the eyes of our hearts.

Yes, your heart will be damaged along the way. Yes, you'll feel many things—some will be good and some will not be so good. But if you stop feeling your way through life, you can't be fully present in the moment.

True reward is found in taking the risk.

True joy is secured in taking the journey.

True love is discovered in taking the leap.

Your heart is where you'll experience all the highs and lows of achieving your dreams. The key is to feel it fully without letting the interruptions distract you from your goal.

The Proposal

It was finally time for me to propose to Sophia, and I needed to talk it out with my future (so I hoped!) father-in-law. It was a bit of a sell to him because Sophia and I had been broken up for a year, had gotten back together, and now were planning to get married. He was a little confused, but he knew our hearts and could see the love we had for each other. He gave us his blessing, as did my parents. We couldn't have been happier.

I really wanted the proposal to be a special moment. I figured I had only one shot to get it right. I wanted Sophia to remember this night forever.

All of our friends and both our families knew about the proposal, but Sophia had no clue. I planned it very carefully and wanted everyone to be there. A friend lured her to the church with the excuse that she had a meeting with our pastor's wife, and Sophia fell for it.

One of the perks of being on the church staff was I was able to use the church facilities to plan for the proposal night. This was a good thing because I didn't have extra money to rent out a facility. The church is also where Sophia and I met, so there were layers of meaning to my decision to propose to her there.

All the lights were out when Sophia arrived, except for a spotlight that was shining on a stool with a single rose on it. I began singing Brian McKnight's "Back at One" to her as she walked down the aisle. It was one of our favorite songs.

Sophia was crying by the time she got to the stool. I had her sit with her back to the sanctuary. She had no clue all our friends and family were there watching. As she sat down on the stool, a video of our journey together started playing. We loved taking pictures along the way, so there were a lot of fun memories for me to stitch together.

Once the video finished, I had the lights come up. Sophia then realized everyone was there with us. I got down on one knee and proposed. (She said yes!) Afterward, we had a huge party at the church to celebrate our engagement. It was a moment I'll always remember.

A Big Wedding

Sophia and I chose May 15, 2004, as our wedding date. We wanted a big wedding. In addition to our families, we invited the whole church. We saved as much money as we could for our wedding. Her parents paid for most of it, but my mom helped a bit too.

After all the planning and preparation, our day finally arrived.

There were a lot of people in that room. I was nervous. I'll never forget what Sophia looked like in her wedding dress. As she walked down the aisle, I kept telling myself just how lucky I was to have been given such a gift. She was the only thing that mattered in the whole world in that moment. She had captured my heart so many years ago.

Our wedding was exactly what we'd hoped it would be. There were a lot of family and friends there, which made it even more special for us. Nearly eight hundred people stayed for the dance at the reception. It was one of the best days of my life.

If there is one word I could use to describe that day, it would be *perfect*. It was a new chapter for both of us, and we were thrilled to be doing life together — forever. When you are young and in love, there really is little concern for the things that seem to weigh heavier as we get older. We were together, and that was all that mattered.

Follow Your Heart

People talk a lot about following their hearts. Some people refer to it as following your bliss. I think they are talking about a deep happiness that comes from things we can't control and possess. In a sense, our hearts can't be controlled. Our feelings rise up from out of nowhere, and we are drawn to follow their lead.

To follow our hearts is to make ourselves vulnerable—open to experiencing joy and pain, peace and war, and even to being complete as well as being broken. We're never sure what will come next, the joy or the pain, but we know that a life that doesn't follow the heart is not as full or satisfied as one that does.

Sophia and I dated for several years, and there were many twists and turns. But we were determined to be together. It was the best way we knew to live as we pressed forward into the future we dreamed of, and it's the reason we found true love.

It's risky business engaging your heart and moving in the direction of your dreams. Even my dream relationship, one that resulted in marriage, had its share of pain mixed with joy. When pain comes to the heart, we have two options: We can shut down our pursuit of our dream, or we can face the pain and move forward. When Sophia and I hurt each other, we could have shut down our dream of being together. Instead, we focused on the endgame and dealt with the pain by choosing to forgive. Forgiveness is what kept our dream of being together alive. We had to choose to follow our hearts and to love. Choosing love is the road to life—and life in abundance.

Life presents a variety of circumstances. Sometimes it comes as obstacles that can distract us from our true purpose and derail us from discovering the passion that rests within each of us to live a life of significance. Sometimes life comes at us in such a way that we can't escape who we were created to be.

In all things, we must remain determined to rest our hope in the simple, overused, and underpracticed discipline of following our hearts into the destiny we dream of. Discipline may seem like an odd word to use when talking about following your heart. Discipline simply means you've predecided that your default mode of living will rest within the desires of your heart.

When you live that way, you will find the strength and determination to overcome any distraction and live into the full meaning of who you are, who you were created to be, and whom you were created to love.

I'm an advocate of protecting the heart. Your heart is your real set of eyes. What I mean by that is your heart can help you know which choice is right and which is wrong even when you can't reason your way through a situation or experience. I had no way of knowing at the time how connected my life would be to Sophia. Had I not married her, I would have missed a huge part of my destiny. Follow your heart to pursue your dreams. It is essential.

Chapter 2

A Crutch to Carry Us Through

Hard times are periods of preparation.

Love is pure and untainted—until life gets in the way. Then it becomes a sticky mess.

Sophia and I were absolutely in love with each other. There was no doubt about that. We were young, married, and ready to take on the world. After our amazing honeymoon in Mexico, we found ourselves right in the middle of life.

Sophia started college to study early-childhood education. She wanted to be a teacher. Anyone who knew her could see that loving on kids was her passion. Sophia was amazing with kids, and they loved her. That career path was a perfect fit for her.

But life was messy for us. We didn't have enough money for Sophia to continue on with school, so she dropped out. It was a tough decision. We made it believing there would be a time in the near future when she would be able to return to school and finish her degree. We both felt that it was the responsible thing to do at the time—a mere postponement, not a derailment.

In the meantime, Sophia took a job as a nanny. It didn't pay much, but the family offered us our own living space—two rooms in their basement. We shared the family's kitchen and bathrooms. Although it may sound like the perfect setup for newlyweds strapped for cash, I felt awful about it. I felt like a failure because I couldn't provide a home for my wife. We got married and immediately had to move in with someone else. I wanted us to have our own place. But this is where we started our life together.

When that opportunity ended after about a year, we still weren't financially ready to move out on our own just yet, so we moved in with Sophia's parents. This was another tough choice for me at the time. I wanted to be able to have a place of our own, but I knew we needed to be financially stable before we could do that. Looking back now, I realize this time was an opportunity for Sophia's parents to have two more years with their daughter. I'm so happy we did that, but at the time I felt like a loser for not being able to provide for Sophia like I wanted.

Infected by Generosity

When I married Sophia, I gained a wonderful wife—as well as her school loans and credit card bills. All in all, it amounted to about $13,000 of debt. That's a lot, especially when our combined income wasn't much more than $29,000 a year and our credit was terrible.

I remembered something I had heard before Sophia and I got married. In 2002, during the time Sophia and I had broken up, I went to church to hear a guest speaker. I was really struggling at that point in my life, and I was looking for something—anything—to give me hope and purpose. I had hoped this speaker would speak about courage or trust or even trials. Instead, he came to talk about money. It wasn't exactly a topic I was hoping to hear about that day. Nevertheless, his message sucked me in, and it's what I needed to hear.

Often what we need to hear comes in the most unlikely places and in the most unexpected ways. This speaker talked about money in ways I had never considered. I had learned about giving at the age of twenty and started giving back then. I'm sure I'd picked up bits and pieces of these truths over the years, but this message seemed to connect the dots. It sparked something in me and completely changed my view on money and generosity. I don't even remember one direct quote from this message, but at that moment, I made a choice. I told myself I would do whatever it takes not to be poor and to help others with whatever I have. I didn't know how. I even doubted if it was really possible, given my financial situation. In spite of every practical reason that showed I had no way to help others or be financially stable, my decision to live my life in a generous way was a major turning point for me. I looked at life differently after that. I saw opportunity.

That decision set me free from the expectations of others to earn so I could spend. Instead, I made a commitment to invest in the things that would last forever by becoming generous with every part of my life. Now I needed to start applying this new life lesson. It was then that something from the Bible caught my eye. It was a passage that spoke of how Jesus is preparing a place for His bride (His people) to live once this life is through. I figured that if Jesus was doing that for His bride, I should do no less for mine! So I set out to settle my debts and prepare a life for my bride.

Sophia and I decided—together—to start chipping away at our debt. We paid as much as possible on the smallest amount of debt to start paying off bills as quickly as we could. I found credit offers that allowed us to consolidate debt and move it to a much smaller interest rate. This allowed us to pay off the debt faster.

It took a few years to get out of debt, but it was worth the effort. It was a crucial time for me to stick with our goal even when it was tough. I wanted to do whatever it took to be a good steward of what we'd been given. I also wanted a better life for both of us. Earlier in my life, it felt impossible to achieve being debt-free because I had no vision for the future. However, I was in a different place now and had a completely different picture of my future.

Sophia and I were both committed to getting out of debt. I was probably a little more obsessive than Sophia, but she was completely on board. It wasn't easy. I was working at the church and driving a truck. That consumed six days (or more) every week. Sophia worked part-time as a teacher and also at a day care across town. She would drive all the way across town just to be with the kids for an hour. Because gas prices were so high at the time, I told Sophia it was counterproductive and costing us more than it was worth. She was spending more money in gas than what the day care paid her for the hour she was there. But Sophia loved those kids and was passionate about what she did. We both chose jobs we were passionate about that paid so little, which is why we both worked more than one job. We knew that if we could get the debt out of our way, we could live the generous life we dreamed about and envisioned together.

Because our time together was limited due to our work schedules, many times our "together time" involved serving in the programs we loved at church. I think Sophia and I enjoyed being together in that way because we didn't need a lot of money to serve. But when it came time for fun, we always grabbed a coupon. I kid you not. Everything we did, we had a coupon for so we could do it at a discount price. Sophia was really good about finding coupons and looking for deals. The crazy thing is I got so used to using coupons that I still use them to this day even if I don't have to in the same way I did back then.

Changing Myself, Changing Others

It was during my financial struggles when I really started to think more like an entrepreneur. I got a job at UPS right out of high school. It didn't last long. My dad commented regularly how working hard for a good company could take me far up the ladder. I completely understood what he was saying, but I didn't share his perspective. I didn't want to build someone else's future by working for that person. I had a desire, even then, to create something out of nothing.

I didn't know where my business interests would lead me, but I knew there was a desire in me I had yet to fully understand. I wanted to help people transform their lives. And Sophia wanted to help children know they were loved and that they mattered. Our passions worked well together, and eventually those would come together in a very special way. Only neither of us knew it at the time.

People who study personal change and organizational change know how important perspective is to creating momentum. If you can't see your situation for what it is, then you don't have any chance of recognizing what needs to change, let alone see how to change.

Change isn't easy. Before I could help others change, I had to change myself. If I weren't able to adjust my own behavior to create a better life for myself, how could I possibly inspire others to do it?

One of the most powerful things I learned was how I could start helping people with what I had and how I could make a difference now in my current circumstance. We're taught we have to be comfortable and have a lot of money in order to help someone and that we need to have all our ducks in a row, but that day never comes. Giving is more than giving finances, although that is a part of it. Giving is through action as well. As I applied those principles in my life, it really changed who I was and made me a better person. I found this gold mine I never knew existed: helping people. We often have our own ideas of what happiness looks like and how we should go about getting it. It was a defining moment in my life when I learned there is a whole other view of life I hadn't seen before.

Making Our Time Count

Sophia and I didn't have our own place for most of the time we were married. At age twenty-seven, more than three years after we married, we were finally in a position where we could afford our own apartment. It wasn't much, but it was ours. It was the first time we had a place we could call our home. I felt a little embarrassed that it took so long, but we were so excited that none of those details mattered.

Because I was working several jobs, I had about one day a week at home. Working at the church involved driving six hundred miles each week back and forth between two campuses, along with all the other activities and programs I was required to be at as a paid staff member. In addition, I drove a truck around town. When it was time for my day off, I was flat-out exhausted. The only thing I wanted to do was stay home.

I'm sure Sophia probably got tired of staying home on the one day off we had together, but I was always so worn out and just wanted to relax. One of my favorite things to do on my day off was watch movies. I'm sure Sophia didn't like watching movies as much as I did. I know she probably wanted to go out. She probably got tired of eating the same things and doing the same things. But if she did, she never said anything or showed any frustration. She simply loved being with me. I wish I understood then just how valuable our time together really was. I might have been a little more creative, a little more intentional, a little more interested in making the most of our time each week.

Start Where You Are

The hardest part about going through this season of life was feeling like we were so far behind other people. I had friends who had good jobs and were being promoted, making a lot more money, and living what they considered to be the good life. I often found myself caught up in moments of frustration wondering when my break was coming.

Hope was hard to hold on to. But it's hope that we needed because we needed its assurance that greater things were ahead. Believing there is something more, something better ahead, is where we find strength to push through our darkest moments. There are a lot of things we don't see, but we just have to allow our story to play out.

I was leading praise and worship at the church, but it wasn't exactly a career in music like I'd hoped for. My longtime dream of a music career was certainly fading. I wondered how long I'd have to pay my dues before my big opportunity would come. I often thought about how long it would be before I called it quits on my dream or at least came to grips with the idea that this may be as good as it gets.

All of those feelings and thoughts could have broken me. I could have fallen into the trap of following the advice so many people gave me: Go find a good job, work hard, and let the company take care of you. But if I had followed that path—not that there is anything wrong with that—I would have given up on something that was already set in motion for me. Our struggles in life prepare us for what's coming next.

Sophia and I lived our married life in ways that many people I'm sure thought was less than perfect. We did what we had to do to get out of debt so we could set ourselves up to be even more generous in the future. We delayed our desire to have our own place until we were financially ready. We invested our time—what little spare time we had—in serving others and spending it with each other. Those were hard days, but they were good days. It wasn't comfortable, but in a way it was just as it should've been for us because it caused us to grow. Comfort leads to complacency and can rob you of reaching your potential. Discomfort may be more challenging but leads to a far more satisfying life. Looking back, I now realize just how happy I was during that time.

The freest way to live is to not be obsessed with what others think about you and your life decisions. I decided to not make popular decisions because they are popular, to not make comfortable commitments because they are expected, to not give in to the expectations of others simply because it is the path of least resistance, and to fight to move toward the direction the eyes of your heart know is true and pure. Clarity comes in following our hearts and the desires that have been placed within us. More often than not, hard times are preparing us for what's ahead.

Start where you are and stop worrying about what other people think about you and your situation. You have been given the responsibility to live your life. I think we give up too much when we subject ourselves to cultural norms that have no meaning and won't last forever. Opposition can either bring you down or mold you and shape you into something better. A lot of people let the hard times bring them down and don't realize God is doing something unique in their lives through these times. No one was going to elevate Sophia and me as examples of two perfect people living a perfect married life, but we were happy and in love. If we kept ourselves connected to each other, we had a peace, hope, and love that was pure, inviting, and promising. We clung to the things that were important, like investing in one another and in others, and didn't allow ourselves to focus on what others might think or say. Hope was a crutch that carried us through these hard times, and that's all we needed.

Chapter 3

Unexpected Hope

Don't allow the dark moments in life to distract you from what matters most.

Sometimes we are so bent on what we think is best for us that we miss what is right in front of us. We sometimes fail to realize there is a grand plan at work. Before I was ready to experience my highest moments, I had to face my darkest days.

Sophia was born with a congenital heart defect. Just days old, she had her first heart procedure. She had another heart procedure at the age of seven. Otherwise, the rest of her life was mostly unaffected by her heart condition. It didn't inhibit her ability to do anything she wanted to do. There were regular checkups with the doctor and an ongoing prescription-medicine regimen. But outside of that, everything seemed normal. There was nothing in her family history that could've predicted a severe heart problem, and there was nothing in her monitoring that suggested anything amiss. The doctor was pleased.

I innocently thought the doctors had fixed her heart issues in her childhood, so I didn't think much of it—until things started getting worse for her.

Something Wasn't Right

The first major medical scare we experienced as a married couple was in June 2005. I can't remember the exact day, but Sophia knew something wasn't right. I could see it on her face. She kept saying her heart was beating faster than normal.

We went to the hospital, and they clocked her heart at more than two hundred beats per minute. That was fast—too fast for someone who was in a normal state of motion. It was later determined that Sophia was experiencing atrial flutter.

The doctor let us know he expected this to happen and that it was fairly normal for someone with Sophia's heart condition and previous surgeries to have this kind of complication. He introduced the option of implanting a pacemaker to keep Sophia's heart in rhythm. He also told us she might need another heart surgery in the future and even possibly a heart transplant someday and that it was dangerous for Sophia to have kids.

At that moment, Sophia and I broke down and cried in his office because we had no idea this was in our future. That day changed everything for us.

We were certainly not aware that Sophia might need to have a pacemaker or another heart surgery as she got older. We also didn't realize it could be dangerous for her to have kids.

The doctor didn't want to implant a pacemaker just yet. He preferred to wait until Sophia was a little older and try other ways to manage her symptoms until surgery was absolutely necessary. We were willing to do whatever was needed and trusted the judgment of the doctor on this decision, so we waited and continued to monitor her heart closely.

We spent most of 2005 through 2007 in and out of the hospital dealing with Sophia's worsening heart condition. This was an interruption in our lives that neither of us expected or wanted. I didn't know it at the time, but that first episode in 2005 was the beginning of some very bleak times in both our lives and our still-new marriage.

Sophia and I did everything we could to get her condition under control. Being people of faith, we prayed for a miracle. That may sound foolish to some. You may think that medicine is medicine; don't confuse it with prayer. But for Sophia and me, prayer was a language that was familiar and helped us stay connected to each other and the hope we desperately needed.

When life comes at you hard, reason and intellect can become a refuge. You can disconnect from the emotion of the situation and try to see it objectively, but I think you are only fooling yourself. Unexpected events like this one—that make you dance on the line of this world and the next—are full of emotion. Prayer is simply a response to that emotion. It is not a sign of giving up. Rather, prayer is laying claim to your belief that things can change for the good.

In the midst of all the visits to the doctor's office and hospital, we were both missing a lot of work. That meant we weren't bringing in a lot of money, which added a new dimension of stress to an already-stressful situation. We weren't making a lot of money to begin with, and we certainly didn't have a big pot of money somewhere we could use in lean times. We had to work if we were going to make our family budget.

Whatever It Takes

Sophia had another severe heart episode the second week of December 2007. It caught us by surprise. I guess we thought the issue would just correct itself and go away. But it didn't, and this one showed us just how serious things were getting.

It was a Sunday, and I was leading worship at church—an hour and fifteen minutes away from home. I got word that Sophia was being rushed to the hospital by ambulance, so I left in a hurry to be with her. On my way to the hospital, I got pulled over for speeding. The cop was clearly angry at me for speeding and didn't want to hear any excuses. I told him my wife has a heart condition and was rushed to the hospital in an ambulance. He asked me if she was dying and I tearfully said, "I don't know." I continued to elaborate on my story, but it didn't stop him from yelling at me and handing me a hefty ticket. I just knew I needed to get to my wife. This time, Sophia was in the hospital for a week.

We tried to make things as normal as possible while in the hospital and trust that everything was going to be okay. You don't always know you are making a memory when you are just living day to day, but there are so many times I look back on now and treasure. I remember watching my first episode of *SpongeBob SquarePants* in the hospital with Sophia and just laughing and laughing (although Sophia didn't seem to like it as much as I did).

By the time Sophia was released to go home, we were both exhausted. All Sophia wanted to do was take a hot bath and relax so she could sleep through the night.

December is a cold time in Milwaukee, but we rarely turned the heat up above sixty-eight degrees because of the heating cost. As I tried to get a bath started for Sophia, it didn't take long to realize the water wasn't heating. I checked the heating unit. It was on, but it wasn't working. It seemed to me like one more thing that could go wrong did. Sophia started crying in the tub because the water was cold. I hated seeing her suffer, and I felt helpless. I had no control. I really wanted to comfort her, and she was in tears from the long week. So I did the only thing I knew to do: I started boiling water on the stove to dump into the bathtub until there was enough hot water for her to have a warm bath. That hot bath meant everything to her.

The Hope of a New Year

We were back at the hospital again within thirty-six hours of Sophia's being released. She was experiencing pain just twenty-four hours after getting out of the hospital, and she stayed up all night. She was crying because she was in so much pain and couldn't breathe very well.

Sophia called the doctor's office that night, and they told her there could be several things causing her discomfort. They explained she should monitor her symptoms overnight and call back in the morning if things didn't improve. She spent most of the night crying from the excruciating pain. I tried as best I could to comfort her.

I think Sophia's tears were also from exhaustion. She just wanted this whole thing to be over. I did too. I was pretty frustrated at this point and angry about what was happening. She had just come home a day ago. What could it be now? We thought they fixed everything. They did all these tests to show that she's good, and then this happens again. I wanted to go back to a normal life, one that didn't include countless doctors visits and surprise trips to the hospital. It took everything in me not to spit anger at God. I knew God could do something, and He wasn't. I didn't understand it. It wasn't what I had in mind for our life together.

When Sophia called the doctor's office in the morning, she was told to come in right away. But when I went out to help get her in the car, I couldn't get out of the driveway because it had snowed that night. I ran to the neighbors' house and pounded on the door. I asked them to help me shovel and push my car out. They pushed us out, and we rushed to the hospital. We later found out that Sophia's pain was from a blood clot in her lungs.

At this point, it was getting close to Christmas, and I started getting scared we might have to spend Christmas in the hospital. Neither of us wanted that. We just wanted to go home. I remember driving to church one morning and praying, *God, please get her home for Christmas.*

Before my fear became a reality, I got a phone call from the doctor on Sunday, December 23, 2007. He had decided to release Sophia. I was going to be able to bring her home that afternoon. We were, in fact, going to be able to spend Christmas together in our home. I was so excited and felt like this was an answer to our prayers.

It's easy to focus on the things that don't last forever and miss the things that do. I hated the idea that Sophia had to keep going back and forth to the doctor and hospital. I didn't want her to live like that. But at least we were able to be together at Christmas. They may not have been the best memories, but they were *our* memories. As painful as it is to see your wife suffer, I certainly didn't want Sophia to think she was alone. I wanted to help her carry the weight of her suffering and comfort her as best I could.

Sophia and I really needed 2008 to be a year of progress and better news. Every year since 2005, life—with the endless medical surprises—had become darker and darker. We needed a turnaround year. We needed to know that the situation was going to get better. We needed hope.

When I woke up on New Year's Day, I was feeling really broken. I did everything I could to ignore the feeling throughout the day, but it didn't go away. When Sophia fell asleep that night, I snuck out to my car and drove around. I broke down in tears and bawled like a baby. I needed to vent my frustrations. I knew I had to let it go. I couldn't keep it bottled up inside.

Sometimes you need to give your frustrations over to God and accept the things you cannot change. I was really discouraged about what was ahead. The things we believed and hoped for weren't coming to pass, even financially. I had quit my trucking job because I was so tired of working two jobs and because I wanted to be there for Sophia during this time. I started questioning if this was going to be the rest of my life. I felt like there's got to be something better than this. Nothing was lining up with what I thought was going to happen. I needed a fresh perspective and a refilling of strength and hope to keep moving forward because dark times are inevitable.

There is simplicity in letting go. You are able to put whatever it is behind you, breathe a sigh of relief, regain your strength, and then walk toward what's ahead.

Neither of us could have anticipated that 2008 would be our last year together and that this was the last Christmas and New Year's Sophia and I would share.

Ten Days

The same doctor who wanted to push out the pacemaker procedure a few years encouraged us to begin seriously considering that as the next step in Sophia's treatment plan. We were ready to do anything at that point. We just wanted this nightmare to end.

Nothing is impossible for those who believe and have faith. We were not happy with the natural world, but we knew there was always a greater plan being worked out. The surgery was originally scheduled in March 2008 but had to be postponed for a variety of reasons to June that same year. When the June date came, we had to reschedule again due to an emergency situation that involved our doctor. This time it was delayed just ten days.

During this time, we prayed together, and other people prayed for us. We wanted nothing more than a supernatural force to intervene and free Sophia from the need to even have surgery. When you are dealing with realities bigger than you are, it isn't unreasonable to reach for something bigger than yourself. This is the place where hope resides.

Those ten days passed very slowly. The only thing we had left was to pray and dream about a better future. The most beautiful thing anyone can do is dream. Most people stop dreaming because they have too many disappointments, experience too much failure, and allow too much doubt to cloud their sense of hope.

In an effort to take her mind off of things temporarily, I took

Sophia on a date. We hadn't been able to do that very much. I wanted to make her smile, make her laugh, and remind her that I would be there for her every step of the way. We talked about what we would say to the doctor when this was all over and done with. We dreamed about what we could do once we felt confident the surprise episodes would stop and our life together could get back to some sense of normal.

I tried to encourage Sophia as much as possible during those ten days. I wanted to take her mind off of the surgery, but the moments when we forgot about what we were about to face came quickly and left quickly. We both understood the severity of what was about to happen.

Choose to Believe

Even though our situation was challenging and sometimes desperate, we chose to live in hope. Focusing on hope allowed our burdens to be lighter. It helped us keep a proper perspective. We refused to be under the situation; we wanted to live above it. We needed to fight from the standpoint that we were going to win rather than be defeated.

We chose to believe the best in the situation. We looked for affirmation that this routine procedure was going to solve Sophia's recurring heart issues that had interrupted our marriage for far too long. We continued to pray and asked others to join us.

Our efforts to remain positive and depend on each other brought us a great deal of joy. We can sometimes be so jaded that we scoff at the idea of believing in anything but ourselves, but belief is much more likely to bring happiness than sorrow. I would much rather be guilty of looking at life through the window of possibility than standing at the crowded doorway of hopelessness.

I didn't want to be in this situation. Sophia didn't want to be in this situation. Nevertheless, that is where we found ourselves. That is what we faced. We could've chosen to allow it to eat away at the precious time we had with each other. We could've allowed it to distract us from the gift of time and presence we could give each other. Or we could choose to keep what was most valuable—hope—always before us and make the best of our time together. We chose the latter.

Chapter 4

A Long Good-bye

Hope will carry you when everything falls apart.

I remember flipping through the TV channels a month before Sophia's surgery and landing on the story of Jeremy Camp, a Christian-music artist who had lost his wife to cancer just a few months after they were married. It changed him and his ministry forever. I wondered what I would do if something happened to Sophia. At that moment, I hoped with every ounce of faith in my body that nothing would ever happen to her. I didn't know if I could handle it. I prayed (almost pleaded with God) that Jeremy's story would not become my story.

Praying for a Miracle

I had to lead worship the night before Sophia's procedure. I wanted her to come with me so we could at least spend some time together while we drove back and forth from Milwaukee to Beloit. I also wanted us to sing worship songs together. I needed to make sure I didn't lose a grip on the faith that was keeping us together in the midst of the chaos. I also hoped that someone there would pull us aside and pray over us. Sophia came with me, and we got to sing together. But no one offered to pray for us, and that hit me hard. I wondered if God was paying attention at all or if He even cared.

As soon as we got home, we collapsed on the couch from the sheer mental weight of the situation. I grabbed Sophia's hand and we prayed one more time that a miracle would somehow still happen and we wouldn't have to go to the hospital. We were both worn out emotionally and physically, so we decided to go to sleep.

I woke up the next morning to Sophia's cries. She was now verbalizing what I was thinking but too scared to ask: *Why—in the midst of our faithfulness—had she not been healed? How much more would we have to endure before the tide changed direction and good things started to happen? When would the good news come?*

I was so distraught. I had to leave the room and go to the living room because my heart was just broken for her. If I could have done anything in that moment to comfort Sophia, I would have, but I couldn't. I hated feeling completely helpless.

A Quick Kiss

On the way to the hospital, Sophia called her family to tell them she loved them. Those were difficult calls to make. We were both scared, but I tried my best not to show it. I wanted to be strong for Sophia. I didn't want to give her any reason to doubt or be fearful in a weak moment.

I remember what she looked like in her hospital bed before the operation. She looked so scared and helpless. We laughed. We cried. We prayed.

I didn't want to leave when they came to take Sophia back for surgery. I told her I would see her later, and I gave her a quick kiss in an attempt to pretend all of this was normal. In reality, I was a mess. I had told myself to play it down and act like all was well, because then it would be, right? If I acted scared, it might trigger all the worst-case scenarios. That quick kiss was my way of acting like everything was fine.

But it wasn't fine. As soon as I left the room, something didn't seem right. I felt like I should go back in the room and say good-bye and kiss her passionately with all the love that was in me. But I didn't. I went to work instead.

I know it may sound heartless that I went to work during Sophia's surgery, but I had just taken a job at The Cheesecake Factory as a server a few weeks before, and we needed the money. Life doesn't just stop when these things happen. But I couldn't think straight. It was evident on my face. I couldn't get my mind off Sophia in surgery. I suddenly realized I couldn't work, so I left. And I never went back. I couldn't because everything changed after that day.

A Startling Turn

The surgery was supposed to take four to six hours. It took twelve. That was a long time to wait and agonize over how the surgery was going. When it was finally done, I got to see Sophia. I tried to speak words of encouragement to her. I wanted her to be strong. I knew she could hear me even if she couldn't respond or stay fully alert.

The hospital had rooms for family members to sleep in. I was exhausted from all the waiting and anticipation, so I took a bed and crashed. I was awakened by the ringing phone. A nurse was calling, letting me know that Sophia had woken up and was asking for me. I ran as quickly as I could to her room, but she had fallen back asleep. Something wasn't right; I just wasn't sure what it was yet. I went back to my room.

Then things turned upside down after that. Sophia was rushed for an emergency follow-up procedure. Later, the doctor explained that her heart had failed just after I visited and they'd had to resuscitate her and take her to surgery immediately to put her on an artificial heart. The only remaining course of action was an immediate heart transplant. What was supposed to be a routine procedure quickly escalated to a life-and-death scenario. I made some phone calls. Several churches had us on their 24-hour prayer lists. If medicine wasn't going to cure her, I was sure prayer could. The group of family and friends in the waiting room kept growing. There were probably a hundred or more people there, showing their support for Sophia. Their love and devotion was amazing.

When we weren't talking, we were praying. And when we weren't praying, we were trying to encourage one another. It was a beautiful picture of how community should work.

Other people in the waiting room heard us talking and praying together. Timid parents who didn't have much support for their own situation approached us to explain what they were going through and asked us to pray for their children. And we did. We kept hearing good news coming from those others we were praying for. That just encouraged us to continue to pray for Sophia.

Parking Lot Prayers

Eventually, there were so many of us praying in the waiting room that I suggested we move to the top of the hospital parking structure, where we would have more room. The sun was going down and darkness was settling in. People came every night to pray the next several days, but there were more people there that night than any other night. We were praying and singing worship songs together. We still hoped and believed for a miracle. After we finished, we looked up and someone noticed what unmistakably looked like a pink heart in the sky. Many of us broke down in tears. I was looking for anything to grab onto and bring hope at that point. I wanted to believe that heart-shaped cloud was a sign that Sophia would be healed.

I know now that was not the plan. Sometimes we don't understand why things don't work the way we want them to, but I'll never forget that cloud in the sky that night. We don't always get what we want or what we'd expect, but there are still signs of hope all around us. Many times, we are left with no explanation for unforeseen tragedy. It doesn't make sense, and we don't know why. That heart-shaped cloud has since taken on a new meaning and has a lot to do with why my organization is called Sophia's Heart.

Two Long Weeks

Sophia made it through the emergency surgery, but she never woke up. We continued to pray. I wasn't able to stay at the hospital around the clock. It was too much for me emotionally, and I needed rest and a break from the trauma. But mostly, I was right by her side.

Sometimes I would get weary of praying. I just didn't have anything left in me, so I did the only thing I had left in me to do.

I started singing.

As I sang, the nurse noticed tears from Sophia's eyes. She tried to encourage me by telling me Sophia could hear me and knew my voice even if she couldn't verbally respond. Her tears meant so much, for those were our only communication since I gave her that quick, passionless kiss before she went into surgery two weeks before.

Those tears connected us once again. I felt like those tears spoke the good-bye I was prompted but failed to give before Sophia was taken away to surgery.

It was a long, long two weeks.

The Call

I had gone home to get some sleep around 3:00 a.m. because we were praying and I was exhausted. The doctor called me at 7:30 a.m., which wasn't unusual. She called often with status updates and also to listen to me and respond to any questions I had. So I just assumed this call was like any other. When I answered, I noticed she had a sense of urgency in her voice I hadn't heard before. She asked me to come to the hospital immediately.

I got there as fast as I could. The lead doctor handling Sophia's case met me on my arrival. I could tell he was visibly upset and dreaded delivering the news that there was nothing else left to do. In tears, I begged and pleaded with them to do whatever it took to keep Sophia alive. There was one last procedure to try, and they reluctantly did it. I just knew a miracle was around the corner.

But there was no miracle from that procedure either. They put Sophia back in her room. Friends, family, and church members prayed with me until eleven that night. Throughout the afternoon, the staff checked Sophia's vital signs and looked for brain activity. Each time, the doctor confirmed my worst fear: There were no positive signs that she was reviving. Three or four times throughout the day, the doctor gently asked me if I was ready to let her go. But how could I do that? I wanted so badly to believe that things would turn around.

By late afternoon, Sophia had already lost color. Although she was on an artificial heart that was pumping blood through her body and keeping her alive, her other organs had already shut down. She wasn't breathing on her own and hadn't been for a while. It was time for me to make the decision no one wants to make for his or her spouse, especially a young married man in his twenties. This wasn't supposed to happen. Not now. Not this way.

I finally came to the conclusion that God didn't need me to keep Sophia alive. If Sophia was supposed to live, she would. If it was Sophia's time to die, she would. It didn't matter how sophisticated the medical treatment or strategy. I mournfully signed the papers to take Sophia off life support. That was the toughest decision I've ever had to make.

That call—and what happened next—broke me.

A New Truth

I am a person of faith. I believe miracles do happen. There are plenty of documented cases to back me on this. Trust me, I did the research. I bought a book during one of Sophia's heart episodes that had documented miracles and stories in it. We would read it together during her hospital stays to lift our spirits and strengthen our faith.

We desperately needed encouragement during those times and tried everything we thought would make a difference. Still, sometimes, everything falls apart. When it happens to you personally, though, all the trite responses and pithy explanations are empty. Part of me wanted to believe, but I was tired of believing with nothing to show for it. I wanted a miracle for my wife, and I didn't get one.

I felt cheated. I felt robbed. I was angry and hurt that my precious Sophia had to suffer and die like that. I was riddled with guilt for having not gone back in the room when I felt the nudge to say good-bye when I knew she could still hear me and respond.

Now I had to face the crowd of people whom I was supposed to lead in worship. What would I do? I had to talk to the people who had prayed with me at the hospital. What was I supposed to say? I had to face the fact that I was the only one who would be coming home to our apartment every night. How was I going to do that?

The only thing I had the strength to do was cry.

Twelve years had passed since I saw Sophia for the first time. Now I was about to bury her and somehow try to find the courage to move on without her by my side. I had lived almost half my life with her. Now what?

Our four years of marriage had been rocked with the constant battle of medical complications and the unknown lurking in the shadows. We had overcome so much together, but we couldn't overcome this. I didn't want to let her go.

I sang for Sophia one more time at her funeral. And then it was time to close the casket. I was painfully reminded I would never see her again this side of heaven.

I remember wishing for a miracle even as they lowered the casket into the ground. I just wanted to pull her out of that box and breathe life into her. Her life wasn't mine to give or take, but that didn't make it any easier to watch her disappear. I was so messed up.

This was my darkest moment. For the first time, I couldn't see or grab on to the hope that was in front of me. I was blind to any promise of something better. I was separated from any logic or reason that might comfort me in the midst of this devastating experience.

But as I look back on this moment today, I realize a truth now that I didn't then. Just because I couldn't see it, just because I couldn't feel it, just because I couldn't make sense of it doesn't provide any evidence that hope, restoration, and the promise of good things were not ahead of me.

No one should have to go through what Sophia and I went through. I would have traded places with her in a second. I never wanted to see her suffer, and I never could have imagined she would die so young and unexpectedly. Sometimes we don't discover our purpose until the darkest moments strip us of everything and all we are left with is brokenness and heartache. It is in these moments, ironically, when hope becomes our strength and carries us until we can see again that hope is always in front of us.

Chapter 5

In the Shadow of My Darkest Moments

The power of your belief system will get you out of your darkest moments.

The dark moments will come. The pain will consume you. The brokenness you feel inside will tempt you to believe that any remnant of hope has been torn to pieces. This is how we know we are human; this is what it means to be truly alive.

The challenge of life is not that we must endure pain; rather, it's that we hang on long enough to get to the other side of our pain. It often hits us in a surprising turn of unexpected events and catches us off guard. And when we aren't ready or prepared, it can push us so far away that we feel as if we can't find our way back.

I never saw the darkness coming. It happened so fast that I wasn't sure if I would ever be able to make sense of any of it. I didn't know what to do next.

There were no words that could comfort me in those days. I felt duped. I had prayed, I had been faithful, and I never lost hope that things would get better for Sophia. Now I was driving home to an empty apartment. I was faced with doing life on my own again.

I couldn't find a reasonable explanation as to why the events played out like they did. Nothing seemed to make sense. I couldn't deny that miracles existed. I couldn't deny my faith. But that doesn't mean I didn't want to. Faith held on to me because I no longer had the strength or the will to hold on to it.

An Amputated Soul

When you lose someone you love, it's like a part of you is missing. I started thinking this must be how someone feels when they lose a hand, foot, or other critical body part. I felt as though my soul had been amputated.

It wasn't supposed to happen like this. Not for Sophia. Not for me. Not in this way.

I felt so lost, wounded, and confused. I wanted to press "rewind" and start over. I wanted things to be different.

I wouldn't have worked so much. I would have spent more time with her. I would have told her even more how much I loved her and how much she meant to me. These are the things I thought about over and over again when I no longer had the opportunity to do them. Why isn't it just as easy to do these things when the people you love are right in front of you?

Once Sophia's medical issues escalated, I had quit my trucking job to spend more time with her and manage the seemingly endless string of doctor's appointments and hospital visits. And after Sophia passed away, I decided I couldn't continue working at the church, either. I tried, but I couldn't face leading worship anymore. I didn't have the strength or the energy. My mind just wasn't right. It was too painful to get up onstage and do everything I was doing. At this point, I had no paid position. What was I supposed to do now?

I was not in a good place. And to be honest, I was more than a little mad at God, who I felt had let this happen. Everything I knew to be true was now in question. I can't say I ever stopped believing, but I was tired and exhausted. Belief and faith had left me disappointed and hurting, but I really didn't have anything else to turn to. I didn't know how to make sense of it all. No matter how much I wanted to in my weakest moments, I couldn't deny my faith. It just wouldn't let me go. What we know is true is still true even when it doesn't feel like it is. It has to be. Otherwise, hope is just an empty promise that will never be fulfilled. And that is something I couldn't even begin to wrestle through in the midst of all my pain.

Changing My Focus

I needed to get out of town. Everywhere I went, there were reminders of my life with Sophia and all we had shared. I went on a road trip that included places like Chicago, Baltimore, and Nashville. I needed to get away from it all.

I had never heard of Jeremy Camp before I saw him on TV a month before Sophia's surgery and heard his story. Little did I know that I would face the same tragedy and be forced to handle it somehow. I couldn't believe it. It was surreal.

Knowing my need for encouragement, Sophia's sister's husband in Nashville somehow contacted Jeremy, and he agreed to meet with me. I was blown away that he would even take the time to do that.

When we met, it felt like we already knew each other. It was as if Jeremy knew exactly how I felt and had been right where I was —because he had.

It was while he was processing his own wife's death that Jeremy wrote the song "I Still Believe." Yes, Jeremy knew exactly how I felt. He reminded me that my life was not over; it was beginning again. He told me how the experience of losing his wife changed his focus. Now he spent time helping other people process and deal with the loss of someone they loved, especially a spouse.

I didn't know if that was possible, but I really wanted to believe it was. I was so grateful he took the time to meet with me. He didn't have to, and I'm sure he was busy. But he sure did make me feel like I was important to him. At that moment, I felt as if there were a promise given to me—that my future would be formed out of my experiences with Sophia and what I had been through. It would be a ministry to help others in their brokenness. It was a faint, small, almost impossible thought, but I held on to it with all I had.

Keep Moving Forward

Despite holding on to that promise, I still didn't know how to process this tragedy in light of my faith. I wanted to deny my faith, but I couldn't. In a strange way, I felt that God was mad at me. I wondered if I had done something wrong.

This was a dark part of my life. I could feel myself slipping away. It tainted how I looked at everything around me, and I couldn't muster excitement or joy about anything. I felt as though my mind and body were separated from one another. I was numb.

What had happened to me wasn't fair. It couldn't be explained. There was no way to reconcile recent events in my heart. Nothing added up.

While I never acted on it, there was a point when I thought it might be better to die than to go on. Although I would never do it, I can't deny the fact that those thoughts went through my mind. I completely understand what that depth of pain feels like. Now when I talk to people who have considered or attempted suicide, I have an understanding of the pain they experienced that made them feel hopeless and alone.

Pain does not discriminate between race, class, or creed. I've met successful people and homeless people who have both experienced the desire to take their own lives. I've also heard their stories of how they fought back through the pain because they had a hope there was something better waiting for them ahead. Suicide is never the way to go. It assumes there is no hope. The truth is, hope is always just ahead, even though you can't sense it at times.

Hope has to be real. If it's not, then I couldn't have found my way through the pain of losing Sophia. The paradox is that we must find something to believe in before life punches us in the gut and knocks the wind out of us. As tough as this period of my life was, it would have been much tougher had I not remained hopeful and clung to what I believed with every ounce of my being—and sometimes it clung to me when I was too weak to hold on any longer.

I learned that the power of my belief system could get me out of my darkest moments. Whether you realize it or not, the things you believe have power over you. Your life moves in the direction of what you believe.

The girl who has been told by her abusive boyfriend that no one will ever want her or love her has a choice. If she believes what she's been told, she'll keep coming back to that and likely stay in her current situation. But if she believes she is better than what she's being told and has hope that a better life is possible even though she can't see it yet, she can work toward a better future and find a better relationship where she will be completely loved and appreciated.

If you don't believe you'll get out of debt, you'll stay in debt. The power of what we believe is a force that drives us one way or the other. You can grab on to depression and it will take you straight down, or you can grab on to something that is hopeful and move forward. The things we believe have power over us.

I heard a profound comment once that fear and faith have one thing in common: They both ask you to believe in something that hasn't happened yet. You can either believe something good is coming or believe something bad is coming. Hope operates in the same way. It keeps us on the right track and looking forward to the days ahead in a positive way.

Everyone believes something, whether they acknowledge it or not, so you might as well believe good. Your mind is always thinking about something, whether it's good or bad. You might as well fill it with good so you see better results. People believed for a long time that the earth was flat. And for years, there was a lot of this beautiful world they never saw because they believed something that wasn't true. Until someone believed differently.

Don't limit yourself. Know what you believe, and focus on good things, not the fear of the unknown. You can fear something will happen or you can hope something will happen. I'd rather focus on the hope so I can see positive results and look toward good things. My belief system offered the only safety net available to me when my world was crashing down right in front of me.

It was my faith that was strong when I was weak.

It was my conviction that carried me when I couldn't walk.

It was my endurance that became my salvation.

It was focusing my eyes on the good and taking my eyes off the bad.

You may feel like you want to throw in the towel. You may think there is nothing left for you on this earth. You may have convinced yourself the pain will never ease, the heartache will never end, and the tears will never stop. Whatever you have faced, whatever trial, betrayal, disappointment, or loss, I can tell you with certainty—as someone who has been to hell and back—to keep moving forward. Keep looking and believing for a better day even if you can't see it or feel it right now. If you do, you will find that your desperation will be transformed into something greater, your end will become a new beginning, and your despair will become a catalyst for personal growth and development.

Not the Only One

In a way, pain reminds us that we are still alive. The abundant life we've been promised doesn't come filtered and separate from pain and suffering. It is part of what rounds out our existence.

We don't go looking for it, yet it seems to find us.

We don't ask for it, yet it comes uninvited.

We don't chase it, yet it feels like it is in pursuit of us at times.

You have a choice to make. You can choose to see the world around you with promise and possibility, or you can choose to see limitations and obstacles. How you look at the world around you is what it will become. Your life will move in the direction of what you're focused on. If your eyes focus on the bad things, your life will move in that direction. If your eyes are set on good or hopeful things, you will move in that direction.

It's like driving. If you take your eyes off the road, you will eventually swerve off the road and go in a direction you didn't want to go. When driving your car, you must be intentional to stay on the road if you want to get to your expected destination. The same thing applies in our lives. If you want a life of hope, your eyes must stay focused on that hope—no matter what distractions or difficulties are around you—in order to get there. How you move through life will determine the quality of your life and your ability to find satisfaction and fulfillment.

Hope is the vehicle that you get into that will drive you through your darkest moments.

I know the road ahead will be hard. This won't be the last time I feel lost, alone, and confused. But I will remember that I made it through.

I'm not the only one. There are others who have endured similar—or even worse—pain. And they made it. This encourages me to think that what seems impossible is possible as long as I have faith and patience. Nothing has happened in your past and nothing will happen in your future that God won't give you the grace to walk through.

If we never felt pain, we couldn't fully understand joy.

If we never experienced grief, we couldn't explain comfort.

If we never lost anything, we couldn't know what it means to be found.

I believe life is intended to be an abundant one.

I believe faith is intended to be worked out in real time.

I believe hope is intended to be flowing constantly in my life and in yours.

Nothing made sense at this point in my life. I still felt empty. But I chose to believe that better things were ahead of me. My purpose in life was waiting for me in the shadows of my darkest moments. I was far from feeling put back together again, but I sensed I was headed in a new direction.

Chapter 6

Wrestling with Letting Go

Letting go of bitterness will keep you moving forward.

Children have an amazing way of letting go. It is almost effortless for them. If you ever have to intervene in a fight between two kids over a toy, you will observe a few things: Their emotions run high, there will likely be tears streaming down their faces, and their hearts will be heavy over what seems to them to be a really big deal.

Once they settle down and separate for a minute or two, all of that emotion disappears. They are likely to be smiling at each other again. The relationship is restored, and they are playing together as if nothing happened in the first place.

Children have yet to even realize how bitterness can be so destructive. Their memories are short. They are quick to forgive when they have been wronged and even quicker to let go when they have been hurt.

Come Together

Bitterness can rob us of everything. Sophia's death was tragic and it wrecked me, but I couldn't stay in that state forever. I had to let go of the sadness and depression so I could reach forward to what was in front of me.

The emotions from losing Sophia were overwhelming. I was exhausted from all the years of doctors' visits and hospital stays and having to watch helplessly as she cried at night because she just wanted to have a normal life. She deserved more than that.

The doctors told me she had only a 10 percent chance of dying during this operation. We had tried everything to avoid the surgery, but it was inevitable. Our efforts exhausted our options financially, spiritually, physically, and medically. Nothing worked.

I was shocked from the sudden loss and left with nagging questions I would never be able to answer. Bitterness, anger, and resentment began to fill my mind and started to take root in my heart, which launched me into a deep depression.

Some might say that is normal. Maybe they are right. But what I felt was more than just sadness. It was a darkness that left me wandering without a sense of purpose, mission, or reason to go on.

I felt like I had to put on a face for everyone to cover what was really going on inside. Deep down, I felt my hope was fading.

Take it from someone who knows how hard life can be at times. So many lives have been torn apart because of tragedy. It can devastate you if you allow it to. As much as I wanted to hang on to the bitterness and resentment, I knew deep down it wasn't going to solve anything. I had also read some research on how negative emotions such as bitterness and resentment could lead to other diseases and shorten my life.

I had to deal with this if I had any expectation of reclaiming a sense of normal in my life. If I had not dealt with this depression, it probably could have somehow taken me out. So I began to pray again. I desperately needed help. And this time, I sensed God was trying to get a message through to me. I started seeing a verse, Psalm 46:10, show up everywhere. I didn't understand it at first, and I wondered why I kept seeing this verse wherever I went.

If I was ever going to move forward, I really needed something to come together for me, so I started studying Psalm 46:10. It says, "Be still, and know that I am God." I found a note that in the original Hebrew context, this is the idea of letting go, but not in a simple, loosened-grip sort of way. Rather, it has the sense of a forced release from something that is pulling you downward. It's a vigorous breaking of your grip using extreme force. Wow! I distinctly remember the image in my mind of hanging on to Sophia's casket as she was being buried and my grip was so tight that I was being buried with her. I felt like I couldn't let go. This is a natural response when we are in a situation we can't control or make sense of.

The problem with hanging on for dear life is we won't be able to find new life until we have released ourselves and fallen into what's next. The danger in this is we can't control, predict, or understand what will happen next because when we are in this state, we don't see things as they are. We see everything through a distorted, poisoned, and polluted lens. Our pain is defining us rather than us defining our pain.

But there is another option: We can let go. This was the answer that came to my mind as I read and reread this simple, short psalm. I knew what I had to do: I had to let go and do it with force.

More important, I had to be the one who made the decision. No one could do this for me. No amount of encouragement could have replaced the single action I had to take to find closure and begin the process of healing. I had to force myself to release all the toxic energy that had built up in my body so I could make room for the healing.

Part of the reason I had become so bitter was I wanted justice. I wanted answers. I wanted to know why, and I wanted to know what we could have done differently. It didn't seem fair. Even the answer of letting go didn't seem fair. I felt like I was stuck in a situation that was God's fault and not mine. Sophia didn't do anything to deserve this. I was hanging on so tightly to this you would've thought I expected to get answers that would satisfy and dampen my pain. You and I both know that never would have happened.

I knew, however, that if I didn't let this go, I would forfeit any hope that might still be ahead of me. The cost of hanging on to the bitterness and anger was actually much greater than the cost of letting go. It doesn't make sense, but it's true. It's not logical, but life is rarely rational. It's not easy, but each step forward comes with both risk and reward. You can't have one without the other.

Letting go didn't mean I would somehow forget about Sophia. I could not and would not ever do that. But it did allow me to begin to heal inside and see life differently.

I remember sitting on my bed with tears running down my face and saying to God and myself, *I refuse to let this be the last of me. I refuse to let this define me and poison my future. This will not defeat me.* I would picture myself pounding my hands open and letting go. I had to do this many times throughout the months after Sophia's death, but it finally set me free. The bitterness began to drain from my heart, and happiness and joy took its place. I started seeing life in a new way. The grass was greener and the sky was bluer.

As I look back on this dark time, it amazes me how much my poisoned heart changed my ability to see things and how horribly I viewed things. I'm so thankful for this realization. It saved me and set me free.

Ready for Freedom

I can tell you that nothing magical happened immediately. But over time, I have been able to enjoy life more and more. I'm grabbing hold of new opportunities that would have otherwise been lost. I'm not buried in my bed under my sheets at home, angry at the world and God. Instead, I began to move through the stages of healing because my heart was no longer bound by resentment. I began to wonder if Sophia's life and heart might be able to touch countless others.

When I forced myself to let go, that is when I was able to move forward. Your past and future don't mix. It's either one or the other. If you hold on to your past, your future will only be revisiting that past over and over again. I know it seems hard, and it's not the answer you might want to hear, but take it from someone who has been there.

My life has improved one thousand times over since letting go of my depression. So many people and families are torn apart because of their unwillingness to let go — because someone doesn't want to forgive someone else and move on. Many people tend to think that terrible situations and terrible relationships will somehow fix themselves. They think that emotions like anger and refusing to forgive will bring justice. They won't.

I've made a choice to be free. Freedom doesn't mean I no longer lay claim to my past, especially the part of my life that included Sophia. I will always carry her in my heart. There are times when I just know she is next to me.

The freedom I am referring to means no longer being held back by anything that is keeping me from living my destiny. It means no longer being defined by situations and circumstances that are out of my control. It means no longer blaming myself for all the pain Sophia had to endure.

Instead, I've made a choice to cherish and be thankful for the wonderful times I shared with her. It's not easy. Some mornings I wake up and still struggle with anger and sadness. But my reaction today is much different.

I choose to release those emotions. I choose to exercise gratefulness, which always makes for a better day. With that powerful principle, I was able to remove the roots of bitterness from my heart.

Doing so allowed the seeds of thankfulness and joy to take its place. Since that time, my heart harvested and cultivated those attributes.

The Future Holds Promise

Having hope in front of me got me out of the darkness. It helped me realize I must live moving forward.

The past is a catalyst for who I am today. But I am not living in my past, as the future holds a lot of promise.

I strongly urge you to examine your life and let go, once and for all, of those things that are holding you back. It could be a harmful self-image, disappointments, setbacks, wrong relationships, or anything else that holds you in the pit of your past that might keep you from embracing your present and future.

Become like a child and don't let your heart hang on to those things. Let yourself bounce back with new hope and second chances. The best is yet to come for you. Believe it; it's yours for the taking.

The present is now. Today is your chance to embrace everything and everyone in it and get ready for what's to come.

The present holds the most precious gift for you and me: the chance to love the people in our lives. Some of those people are likely easy to love. Some of those people aren't. It doesn't matter. I would much rather spend the rest of my life loving people than continuing to hold on to the baggage from my past or buy into the idea that suddenly things are just going to change. That never happens.

Whatever you are holding on to, recognize that it has a grip on you.

Whatever has a grip on you, believe you have the power to release it.

Whatever you have released, celebrate that you are ready to move forward.

You will be surprised how beautiful life is when you let go of what you don't understand and can't control. Refuse to let the things you can't control take control of you. Before you can find purpose in your darkest moments, you must be free from the lingering bitterness in your soul that clouds your judgment, disrupts your relationships, and prevents you from seeing the hope that is right in front of you.

Chapter 7

We All Start Somewhere

You can't control where you begin, but it doesn't have to determine where you're going.

Where we begin can be either an anchor or a launching pad.

I'm a midwesterner through and through. This is where I begin, where the story of my life starts. My hometown is Milwaukee, Wisconsin. We work hard, care for the people we love, and generally have a positive outlook on life. The Midwest is the heartland of American industry, the place that built America over the past century or so — at least as long as America has depended on industry as an economic engine.

I am one of six children — fifth in line with four sisters and an older brother. Growing up in a family of our size was an interesting experience. We couldn't even fit in one car. And we never went anywhere quickly. Actually, we didn't go many places at all besides school and church.

I love how I grew up. It wasn't always easy, but I had someone to care for and look after me. And I constantly had someone to play with (or get into trouble with, whichever seemed to be the better idea at the moment).

My dad worked in construction, and much of what he did was dangerous. At one point, he blasted rock underground in the sewer system. He had a few close encounters with death, and a few of his coworkers were actually killed. But my dad considered it his responsibility to provide for his family. He went to work and never complained, even through sickness and injury. The work he did really took a toll on his body, even to this day. He was also laid off multiple times due to the nature of his job and had as many as three jobs at one time. I can only imagine how tired he was most days, yet he always had time for us.

My mom was great with kids and invested a lot in us. She didn't work outside the home because she was raising us, and six kids can be a handful. She was a professional babysitter, and that's how she made money. I don't know why she'd want to add other people's kids to the chaos, but it was more friends for me. I can't remember a time when our home wasn't full of children. Even after an exhausting day of babysitting, cooking, laundry, and other household duties, my mom still took time to read to us and pray with us each night.

Neither of my parents graduated from high school. They met early in life, got married, and started a family. While I'm sure my parents knew that education creates more opportunity, life got in the way and happened quicker than they'd imagined. The responsibility to care for a family at a young age is heavy. Like a lot of people, my parents had to depend on their survival instinct and strong work ethic to make ends meet.

In addition to working hard, my parents taught us to have faith. I can't remember a time when faith wasn't part of my life. Faith has always been part of who I am, and it always will be. For a long time, our family attended the church my grandfather pastored. At best, it averaged fifty people per week. It was a small, nondenominational church located in a rough part of town. There were always break-ins, and it wasn't unusual for one of us to find our car had been broken into while we were in church.

Some of my earliest memories are from church. I've attended a variety of churches over the years, but my first church will always hold a special place in my heart. We were active members in my grandfather's church until I was twelve. This is where my faith began.

Musical Beginnings

I grew up around music. My family used to sing in front of the whole church—all eight of us, just like the Partridge Family. Mom and Dad wrote songs and sang at weddings. Dad was the song leader at the church we attended when I was very young. Mom and my aunt directed the children's choir, so we were always involved in plays, even some leading roles.

Dad always seemed to have a guitar in hand and a song on his lips. He would make a song out of anything. Whether it was time to get up, go to school, or eat, he always said it with a song. We would all harmonize with him. Even when we didn't want to do something, Dad would sing a song and somehow the task at hand became interesting.

When I was five, Dad bought me a small, pint-sized guitar that looked just like his. Although mine was never in tune, I played it like it was. When Dad led worship, he would let me come onstage with him with my little guitar. I would mimic him strumming his guitar and he'd play with me and smile. I loved to listen to Mom sing at church too and would try to match her voice. That is how I learned to harmonize. We often sang as a family when we were together, especially at my grandparents' house. I also played trumpet from fifth to tenth grade.

A Simple, Good Life

For the first few years of my life, we lived in a duplex owned by my grandparents. It had three bedrooms and wasn't big enough to keep us from stepping all over each other. It wasn't until I was about seven years old that my parents bought a single-family home of their own.

We didn't have a lot of extras, but I never really thought about us being poor. The main time we had the sense that we didn't have as much as others was during Christmas. Other kids at school would talk about all the cool gifts they got, and I was suddenly aware we didn't have all those things.

As you can imagine, we went through a ton of food. Some people use the phrase "a ton of food" as a way to describe how they feel after eating too much. But eight people go through, literally, a ton of food. The sheer cost of food—if we purchased it at the local grocery store—would have been overwhelming for just about any family, especially mine. Because my grandfather was a pastor, he had access to a secondhand food shelter nearby that offered day-old food at a significant discount to homeless shelters and other programs that fed the hungry. This is how our family of eight had enough to eat; it was a saving grace for us. The label-less and dented cans made every meal a surprise. The rule was you had to eat whatever was in the mystery can you picked. (We always hoped it wouldn't be beets.)

Being one of six kids, you learn to share everything. Nothing is really your own. This created a "Take all you can while you can" mentality in me. I later learned just how unhealthy living with that mindset is. When "taking all I can" didn't work, I discovered that generosity was the key to getting everything I wanted in life.

Who you become is not determined by how much you have but rather by what sacrifices you're willing to make. Great athletes take care of their bodies and avoid substances and habits that could harm them. Great musicians care for their talents and avoid lifestyles that could prematurely destroy their God-given abilities. Great leaders care for their influence and avoid making decisions that could damage their reputations.

My parents did the best they could with what they knew to do. Their love for us and unwavering commitment to sacrifice for our needs again and again is something I'll never forget. They taught me that whatever is important to you is worth sacrificing for.

The way I see it, my family lived the American Dream. That means different things to different people, of course. To me, the American Dream is less about what you have as it is about who you get to do life with. I think sometimes we confuse the American Dream with what we possess. It's as if there is a power that comes from accumulating things. I think that mentality can be toxic because it takes our eyes off the things that have real value: people and relationships. Things and success aren't the foundation upon which the American Dream exists; families and friendships are. I was part of a family who loved me and wanted to help me have a better life. We loved each other deeply, and this is what mattered most to us.

The Strength of a Family

I can't think of any other place that influences our minds, hearts, and lives more than the homes we grow up in. It's where we first learn how to relate to others, how to care for one another, and — more important — how to depend on each other. That's why it was so difficult when we found out there was infidelity in my parents' marriage. It's funny how one day can change everything. They decided to get a divorce. I was nineteen, and nothing was the same after that. It was tough and a huge blow to the bond our family had built over the years. The pain of the infidelity caused my parents to act differently than we'd always known them. My parents became two individuals acting on their own instead of the supportive team our family needed. I always thought our family was exceptionally tight and had a bond that would never be broken. When it was severed, it took a long time to adjust. Everything I knew was reordered and rearranged.

My parents didn't intend to get a divorce, but things just fell apart over the years. That decision still affects me to this day. There's not a "real home" to go to when I visit Milwaukee, and family traditions around the holidays—or even just being together—aren't the same. The security I found in my family was gone. Home was no longer a place of refuge because both my parents, whom I had depended on, weren't in the house I called home up to that point.

There is never a time when you don't need a parental figure in your life. The home should be a place where you feel loved and covered. When a home is broken, so is that sense of security. My parents' divorce wasn't what I wanted. I wanted my mom and dad to be together, but sometimes life comes at you in the most unexpected ways, even ways you can't understand or process. You just have to do your best to learn from those things and keep moving forward. I needed to deal with it so it wouldn't make me bitter or resentful.

It has been many years since my parents divorced, and we are still coming to a place of healing as a family. But through all the drama and brokenness, we manage to love each other. In fact, our love for each other today is stronger than ever. Divorce divides and leaves people broken, but that doesn't mean things have to stay that way forever.

The split in my family was painful, but nevertheless, my family is still my family. Although it's not the same as it was before, we are slowly picking up the fragmented pieces and putting them back together. I find a lot of strength for today from the environment I called home and the family I called my own growing up. Our relationships still need some healing, but we have looked past each other's faults, and love has helped us overcome. When we get together as a family now, it's fun and obnoxious—in the best sort of way. We may express our love for each other in somewhat unconventional ways, but the love we have is very evident, even when we don't see eye to eye.

Your Future Is Yours

Many people think only those of privilege and money have access to amazing opportunities. I had neither growing up, but some very significant doors were opened for me over the years. What is most important is that while I treasured my past, I didn't let it define me or blind me to the opportunities that came along.

There is power that comes when we free ourselves from our past and open ourselves to greater things. That's what I found when I took those small steps my parents wanted me to take. They knew that just as my past had prepared me in some ways for life, it could also become an anchor that limits creativity and imagination. Where you begin doesn't have to be where you end. Instead, see your past as what has uniquely positioned you to launch forward into great things—things you have yet to see, consider, or dream about.

You can't control who your parents are, how you grew up, or what opportunities you did or did not receive. Instead, remember that:

You are free from your past.

You don't have to become something you are not.

You can't control where you came from, but it doesn't have to determine where you are going.

My family is my family. How I grew up is how I grew up. While it certainly shaped me, I wouldn't say it defines me. It may have planted some seeds—good and bad—that I've either had to cultivate or eliminate as I've grown and matured, but it is not the full measure of who I am or even who I am becoming.

My parents always encouraged me to make different decisions than they did about money, career, and education. They didn't want me to automatically make the same choices they made; they wanted something better for me. My parents knew I had the potential to break free of anything that might hold me back and move toward all I was created and destined to become. I don't even think my parents knew what the right answers were, but the encouragement to make better decisions than they did affected me and made me pursue a different life for myself.

Too many people think that because their parents were alcoholics, drug addicts, or even criminals, they are destined to follow that same path. Many people subconsciously become what their parents were because they haven't been exposed to anything else. What we see growing up does play a huge role in who we become and how we live. Every choice leads us somewhere. The good and bad will add up to how our lives will play out in the future.

Where you came from is important. Don't forget that. Don't let it fade. Remind yourself of it regularly. But don't obsess over it to the point that you repeat what you intended to avoid.

I'm grateful for my simple, midwestern life. Faith, love, and a strong work ethic gave me the foundation I needed to stay grounded for the life I didn't even know was ahead of me. Even though I didn't know what my life would be, I knew there was more for me than what I could presently see, taste, touch, and feel. I decided early in life I wasn't going to be defined by how others perceived me or what limitations were around me. I was going to reach forward into the unknown with the expectation that greater things were ahead.

You can do the same thing. There is more than you can see or know, and all you can do is reach forward into the unknown and search for it. Honor your past, but don't be limited by it. Embrace who you are today and the person you are becoming. And—most importantly—move forward with confidence that who you are is enough. Where you are going in the future is determined by what you focus on. There are bigger and better plans for you than you ever imagined. See it and believe it with unwavering faith, and soon you will be living it.

Chapter 8

The Day I Learned I Could Sing

The way you see the world has the power to shape your present and influence someone else's future.

Have you ever wondered why music is so powerful?

To the songwriter, it's words on a page. To the musician, it's notes on a scale. To the singer, it's words and breath and performance. To the band, it's a puzzle of instruments fitting together in beats per measure. To the producer, it's all that mixed with precision.

Music is powerful not because of the individual pieces but because of how those seemingly unrelated and conflicting pieces come together to make someone feel something. And if the music is good enough, it becomes the soundtrack that captures our emotion, our perspective, and even our deepest dreams at a particular moment in time.

Music is powerful because it has the ability to shape us.

In Just a Matter of Words

I loved music, but it never occurred to me that I could sing, at least not until my dad said I could.

We were on our way home from church. It was a random Sunday. No special occasion. It was Mom, Dad, one of my sisters, and me. I was listening to the music playing in the car, which had captured my attention for the moment.

I leaned forward, just behind the console, and started singing with the music. I didn't care that I was singing out loud. I was just enjoying the moment.

Dad quietly looked over at Mom and said, "Your son can sing."

I hadn't expected that statement to come out of his mouth.

I sat back in my seat and didn't know what to say. I didn't know what to think. I looked out the window and warmth filled my whole body. That seemed like a profound moment, as if time stopped.

I was twelve years old at the time, and my dad was my hero. His statement seemed as if it were a window into my future. It had never occurred to me that I could sing. Being a singer or musician wasn't even on my radar. Dad wasn't necessarily prophetic, but that moment was a defining moment for me. No, the clouds didn't part. A voice from heaven didn't speak. No doves flew out of the sky. (That would have been cool, though.)

I liked the idea that Dad thought I could sing, and I took it at face value. If Dad said I could sing, then I could sing. I think parents sometimes underestimate the power they have to speak into the lives of their children. Take it from me, this kid who believed his dad and whose life took off to fill the shape of those words. This is the power of a parent's words upon a child's ear and future. These words can build up or tear down. And because of this moment, when my dad spoke into my life, I've been acutely aware of how I want to talk to my own children and others around me.

I wish I could tell you that my parents called a talent scout the next day and had someone meet with me immediately. I wish I could tell you that after hearing me, the talent scout signed me to an amazing record deal and I became a legend. But as you can imagine, we headed home after church and went back to our regular routine. In just a few minutes, I would be thinking about any number of things, none of which had to do with singing. I loved the idea that I could sing, but I had no idea where that would take me or what would come next.

Shortly after, I sang karaoke on a stage of a water park we were visiting on a family vacation. That was my first public performance. I was a scrawny kid (who probably looked more like eight years old than twelve) in swim trunks and no shirt, belting out Little Richard's "Tutti Frutti." By the time I was done, the area around the stage was packed and people were cheering loudly for me. I'm pretty sure people were shocked that a young boy could sing like that. As I walked through the crowd after my song, I felt like a million bucks because people were walking up to me and telling me how great they thought my performance was. It was a foreshadowing of something bigger and better yet to come. I just didn't know it yet.

Take the Lead

Two years after Dad declared I could sing, I found myself at the beginning of what I thought would be a long career in music. Fourteen is an interesting age. You're not an adult. You're not a kid. But everyone expects you to act like an adult and still be a kid. (This is why fourteen-year-olds are so confused.)

I was eager to use the gift both Dad and I now knew I possessed. So I did what any self-respecting singer did in high school: I tried out for what is known as the glee club.

This group of elite singers was the best of the best in the high school. I had already envisioned what I would look like singing with this group onstage. I practiced for my audition and gave what I thought was a stunning performance.

My music career had just begun—or so I thought.

There was only one problem. The music coach didn't think I was ready. I didn't make the cut. I wasn't good enough. Even worse, my brother was selected. I may have been good enough for Dad, but I wasn't good enough for a spot on the stage.

I was certainly disappointed by not making the cut at school, and after that, music just fell to the back burner for a time. Then a new youth pastor came to our church. He recognized I had a gift for singing and pushed me to use it. He continued to draw out my musical abilities and bridged the gap in my teenage years before I had a vision for myself. He was grooming me for a music career when I didn't even know it yet. He was a key factor in keeping music as a focus and encouraged me at every turn to keep going.

Once again I tried to pursue what I thought was my next step in my music career. Berry Gordy came to Milwaukee and there was a huge tryout to discover new talent for his record label, Motown. I sang my heart out and was pretty confident I had made the next round—but I didn't. I didn't even make it through the first cut. Where was the "Tutti Frutti" crowd when I needed them?

I may not have made the cut for the elite high school singing group or Berry Gordy, but I did try again. This time I was hoping to sing with the praise and worship team at a new church I started attending. Several years had gone by since the sing-along in the car, but my desire for music was still present just as it was the day Dad told me I could sing.

Up until this point, I'd spent most of my life comfortable in the background. I was eager to be involved in the things that mattered to me, but I never wanted to take a lead role. Out in front wasn't where I felt most at ease, so I tried out to be a background vocalist. I was so excited when I made the group and was looking forward to using my love for music and singing in a particularly meaningful way. Little did I know what was about to happen next.

One Sunday morning out of the blue, the pastor pulled me aside and told me I would be the lead singer for worship from now on. My eyes grew wide and I became speechless. I was completely frightened because I didn't think I was good enough. I hadn't spent a lot of time onstage in front of people. This was all so new to me and more than a little intimidating. Now I was being asked to take the lead.

I questioned myself, which is probably why I started the first song with my back to the crowd. I didn't want to turn around. I guess I convinced myself that if I didn't see the congregation, they weren't really there. I looked over at the piano player. She was pointing to me to get my attention and motioning for me to turn around and face the crowd. I was too scared to face them. I remember shaking my head and saying no. I really didn't want to, but I knew I had to face my fear head-on. It was time.

Looking back, the sum of my life is just a bunch of people really believing in me and pointing out the talents and abilities I didn't know were there. I'm grateful for all those who were placed in my life who pushed me toward becoming the person I am today.

There will be surprises along the way to your destiny. That's why hope is so important to harnessing the power we need to pull us through our difficult moments. Someone is always going to think that you don't live up to their standards or meet their expectations. It's key you surround yourself with people who recognize your gifts and push you toward your dreams.

What's important to remember is we choose the way we see the world. Perception is everything. If we think the world is closing in, we'll miss the doors and opportunities that are before us. I could've given up when I didn't make the high school glee club or Berry Gordy's record label, but I didn't.

Faith and Patience

From the time I was twenty until I was twenty-eight, I led praise and worship for my church. During that time, I was able to get comfortable in my own skin singing in front of people. I learned how to direct a group of vocalists, connect with a crowd of people, and put musical sets together. These were all invaluable lessons for me. I didn't know it at the time, but I would one day find myself on a very big stage with lots of people watching me and waiting to see if I could capture their attention from the platform. Had I not been through those eight years of training, I wouldn't have been ready to embrace the opportunities I would soon encounter.

Life has an interesting way of unfolding. It seems disconnected and out of sync most of the time. But when you look back, you can see where it connects. I'm always surprised at how connected life really is when looking back at it.

Sometimes people assume that if things don't work out right now, it's not meant to be. We often give up too easily. As a result, we never get to see our dreams come true, which is really unfortunate.

The reason most people never see their dreams come to be is they don't have faith and patience. We must have faith in our ability to do the things we are passionate about. For me, it was having a music career. For you, it may be getting married, getting that next promotion, or finishing your degree. Faith is the muscle we need to see what hope tells us is true, good, and possible.

In addition to faith, we need patience. It was eight years between the Sunday when Dad told me I could sing and the day I sang lead at my church. Between that time, it was a journey that included setbacks and rejection. I was rejected several times by people I thought would embrace me and my talent.

Then it was another eight years after that before I hit the *American Idol* stage. That's a total of sixteen years before I saw my dream of a music career truly begin. It was a long road. Sometimes it was hard to be patient. And believe me, there were times I wanted to give up. Even as I look back on it now, the things I thought were setbacks were actually times of preparation and necessary experiences for my future. I'm so glad I didn't focus on those disappointments or allow them to hold me back.

Unfortunately, some people will miss out on their dreams because they don't have the patience and faith to hang in there until all the pieces come together. Don't give up. Be patient and have faith that your dreams are possible. Just know that some of the things you are doing now are preparing you for what's ahead.

Destiny Is Real

I believe that you have a destiny. I believe I have a destiny. If we don't have a destiny, then we don't have a chance of finding purpose, meaning, or significance. Destiny is the heavenly push that activates our faith and confirms our hope for the good things still to come.

Every day we are living out our destiny. If you give up on your dreams today, then that becomes your destiny for today. Although most people look at their destiny as ten or twenty years down the road, what you do today becomes your destiny for the moment. All these moments add up. Make the choice today to move in the direction of your goals and dreams.

There is still more for you to accomplish. There is still part of your future you have yet to uncover. I believe there is more in this life for you than you presently understand.

The amazing thing is we are all in the middle of some part of our destiny right now; we just don't see it yet. You can't see it because your knowledge of the big picture is limited.

All you know is right in front of you.

All you have to go on is what you have right now.

All you have to lean on is the measure of faith and patience it will take to get you to the next step.

You may be in the middle of pain.

You may be experiencing success.

You may be ready to give up.

You may be ready to take on the world.

Whatever your experience, whatever you are going through, there is an even bigger picture and more to your story that has yet to unfold.

Words shape how we see the world around us. My dad's encouragement allowed me to see a vocal talent in myself I didn't see before. If you think about it, the words we use to describe the world are probably the words that describe what we believe. If we see the world as limited, then our lives will be limited. If we see the world as unlimited, then it will be unlimited.

The words we speak will shape our lives. It will change our behavior and create a life that is greater and more significant than what we presently experience. Even now around my house we always watch what we say to each other. We refuse to be limited by a life—or even worse, a lie—that we created and now believe. Since I've changed the way I talk to others, my life has significantly changed for the better.

Even more, the words we speak have the power to shape the lives of the people around us. You might be the catalyst for someone else to take the next step in realizing his or her deepest dream. It may be a kind word, a warm blanket, or a loving shoulder. Whatever it is, we are instruments in a concert much greater than we could ever imagine. And when we live out of the part of us that gives us the confidence to speak our dreams into existence, we find a strange, unwavering hope that lives outside the limitations of our lives. It illuminates our path just enough to help us take the next step. Your destiny will be found in the words of hope we speak to ourselves and to others around us.

Chapter 9

Out of Place

Embrace your uniqueness and appreciate the beautiful differences in others.

I attended a private school across town until my early teens. The local public school I would have attended was full of gangs and didn't have a great reputation. My parents made sacrifices to give us a better education.

There were lots of wealthy kids at the private school. I didn't have the brand-name clothes they did. I didn't have a brand-name backpack. I didn't wear brand-name shoes. I had the best my parents could afford, and it met the minimum standard set by the school administration.

My parents weren't always able to pay our tuition on time. My mom would get a call from the principal telling her we weren't allowed to come to school because our tuition was past due. I was happy when we didn't have to go to school. Those were great days for me. But my mom would be torn up about it. She was doing her best to keep us out of public school because she didn't want negative influences to take us down the wrong path. I remember hearing my mom crying in her room after receiving one of those calls. Although I enjoyed my days off from school when she got those calls, it hurt me to see her go through that. There were many times when my grandma would step in and pay our tuition.

Every time I had a friend over to my house, they'd expect my house to be huge because we had so many kids in our family. My friends made comments of how shocked they were at how small our house was. Many of them had much larger houses with fewer family members. I think they assumed we were well off because of the school we attended.

I remember my first pair of Nike shoes. My parents bought them off the clearance rack for twenty-four dollars at JC Penney. Until that day, I always wore shoes that weren't name brand, and other kids made sure I was aware of it. I couldn't wait to wear my new shoes to school. The first day I wore them, I kept looking down at them because I was so proud of them. One kid made fun of me because they weren't Nike Airs, which was the hottest thing at the time. My proud moment quickly turned into an embarrassing one. It seemed impossible for me to ever fit in because we couldn't afford to keep up with the trends.

My parents taught us responsibility and that money didn't come easy. We never took anything for granted. One time when things really got tough, my siblings and I overheard my mom crying to my dad because they couldn't afford to buy school supplies, so all of us kids went out and got odd jobs to help pay for our own. We also had to help buy our own clothes in high school. It was times like this I learned that if I worked hard, I could have the things my classmates had.

When you grow up not having a lot of extras, you learn to live without them. In a way, it puts you at an advantage compared to those who grow up in the midst of luxury. They have way more to lose than you do.

Many people think there is power that comes in owning certain things. However, a lifestyle like that can be a deceptive path. It makes us believe that what we possess today will be in our possession tomorrow. Also, at times people find identity in their possessions and lose their true sense of self. Further, it makes us believe that what we possess will last forever.

I'm not against wealth, owning nice things, or even success, but I never want to find myself captive to the desire to have certain things to be happy. That's when I'll stop living out of the uniqueness that was placed inside me at birth. Investing in people is a gift I have to give the world. Living any other way will only leave me feeling out of place.

Learn to Adapt

Eventually, my parents could no longer afford to send me to private school. The local public school was an entirely different experience for me. We didn't live in the nicest part of town, and the public high school I was zoned to attend was in a very troubled area. I went from being just another student in my old school to really standing out in my new one.

My first day, there were kids lighting up weed and throwing things in class. Kids were cussing at the teacher and calling him names. This was my introduction to public school. It was like something out of a movie. Not all of my classes were this bad, but this was a shock for me on my first day.

I'll never forget the girl who stole my lunch my first day. Her name was Wanda. She walked right up to me in class and told me I was going to hand over my lunch to her or she was going to kick my [bleepity-bleep]. I didn't know what to think. But between all the expletives, I figured I'd better give her my lunch. So I did.

Another time, I must've looked at a guy the wrong way and didn't realize it because he threw an orange at my head. It missed me by an inch and smashed against the wall behind me.

Later that year, a guy checked me in the hallway. He got up in my face and threatened me because he said I had disrespected his girl. I didn't even know what I had done. But he told me he'd beat me up if I did it again.

These kinds of occurrences happened every day in this school, and it was all so new to me. I laugh about it now because I was like a fish out of water. My parents had sheltered me my whole life, so much so that I didn't even know how to respond to these situations at first.

On the last day of school, I was walking outside the school and noticed out of the corner of my eye that a black SUV had pulled up nearby. Deep in my gut, I knew what was about to happen. In a matter of seconds, I was surrounded by several guys who were not exactly interested in helping me with my homework. They were just looking for someone to beat up on and have a little "fun." One of the guys smashed an egg against my head and it ran all over the side of my face and hair. He told me I owed him money. Of course, being my nonconfrontational, nerdy self, I tried to reason with the guy. I pushed my glasses up on my nose, pulled a pen out of my pocket protector, and proceeded to investigate the situation at hand. I told him I'd never seen him before and didn't know who he was but that I'd like to make amends of the situation and help him find this person that somehow looked exactly like me. Then someone shouted, "Get him!" in the midst of my bartering. I couldn't control myself anymore. I was so scared of what they might do that I suddenly felt a warm sensation running down my leg. I now understand how fear can overtake bladder control.

That day, I was jumped for the first time in my life, and I had no idea why. I didn't understand. I hadn't done anything wrong. I hadn't offended anyone that I knew of. It just happened, and it all seemed out of this world to me.

Everything was new. I didn't fit in, and I was reminded of it often. But I wanted to make sure I adapted and learned from these experiences so I wouldn't duplicate that year. I didn't want to be the guy everyone picked on; I wanted to be on their side.

At my old school, I was expected to *show* respect; at this one, I figured out quickly that I would have to *earn* respect. If I didn't, I was likely to be pushed around until graduation.

It was a culture shock, but I learned to adapt to people's differences. I saw a whole new world I had never experienced before. My parents were afraid for me to be at this school, but I was happy to be there and loved it more than the private (sheltered) school. Although it came with some hard lessons, it shaped me and forced me to find ways to fit in and appreciate the differences in others.

Appreciate Being Different

My perspective changed when I moved from private school to the public high school. It could have devastated me. Like some of my siblings, I could have dropped out altogether, or I could have begged my parents to let me return to my old school.

Instead of trying to escape feeling out of place, I used it to my advantage. No, I didn't join a gang, start selling drugs, or begin beating up people in the hallway in an attempt to fit in. Instead, I saw the diversity I was thrust into as a way to discover an entirely new culture that operated from a different set of rules than I had ever experienced up to that point.

My education really started when I transferred schools. It was such an eye opener. Until that point in my life, my socialization was split between my church and a Christian school. Now I was in the middle of the real world, where things didn't line up perfectly. This sort of education suited me, and it really shaped me into who I am today.

I watched people, learning what made them tick. I was good at this sort of learning and study. If they gave grades for studying human beings, learning about the great variety of people, language, and behavior I observed every day, I would've aced that course.

I wasn't so good at classroom learning and test taking. Although I managed to graduate, my GPA was embarrassingly low, so I'm not going to share that. In fact, my oldest brother came up with the idea of hiding our report cards from my parents. He threatened us all within an inch of our lives if we didn't go along with it. We would intercept the mail and hide our pink slips, which came every three weeks when you weren't doing well in class. I thought it was pretty funny at first, until my parents found out. All it did was get us grounded. And when my parents grounded us, it was serious. We had to stay in our rooms and couldn't talk on the phone, watch TV, or go outside. We couldn't even go to other parts of the house.

Public school made me appreciate being different. We are out of place only when we don't fit someone else's ideas about what is in and what is out. Feeling out of place isn't that bad. Everyone is — in a way — out of place.

Somewhere along the way, someone may tell you you're not good enough, not smart enough, not talented enough, not *whatever* enough. And if you hear that again and again, you start to believe it. That's when you are most vulnerable. Why? Because you allow yourself to start believing the words other people speak into your life, and those words begin to shape and limit your future. It would be sad for your life to take the shape and go in the direction of those negative words. The greatest tragedy is that we will end up robbing ourselves of the joy that comes from living out of our uniqueness. We will find ourselves believing the words of others and living in a way that is not true to who we are. You are never more out of place than when you're living out of someone else's expectations.

See Differently

Simple is hardly a way to describe life. Why do we expect life to be anything but complex, layered with meaning, and multidimensional?

Anything less denies the mystery of our destiny, something we must learn to live into by feeling out of place at times.

Embrace your uniqueness, even if that means feeling out of place.

Be out of place. Don't try to escape it, run from it, or deny it. If you fail to find the strength that comes from feeling out of place, you may miss out on a great opportunity.

When you let someone intimidate you, you defeat yourself. If you exchange your true feelings and desires for the expectations of someone else, you will rob the world of the real gift you have to offer: you. And that would be a misfortune. When you try to be someone else or live up to someone else's expectations, you won't be able to sustain it. It will gut your being until you no longer remember what it feels like to be you. It is a place where death sets in. There is an advantage in feeling out of place. You learn to see things differently. Some of my greatest heroes changed the world because they saw the world differently. They didn't form to any mold or fit into what society viewed as the norm.

You may feel out of place within the community you live.

You may feel out of step with your friends.

You may feel out of sight to those you want to connect with.

But the greatest gift you have to give the world is yourself.

You were perfectly created. I don't mean you are perfect. What I mean is that you were created with everything you need to step into your destiny if you choose not to conform to anything less than who you are.

When you find your value in the approval of others, you will be on a never-ending journey for your next high. You will always need someone else to tell you how smart you are, how talented you are, or how pretty you are. It is an endless search for someone else to like you, often at the expense of knowing you.

People tend to see and describe things in opposites: big or small, dark or light, tall or short. The problem with seeing the world in opposites is that we fail to see how similar things really are.

I could have continued to believe I was out of place in my new school because of the run-ins with other students I experienced. I could have agreed with them that there was something wrong with me. But if I had, I would have lost the strength to keep reaching forward in the direction hope was taking me. Think about all I would have missed out on if I had given in to their expectations of me and started to see myself as they saw me.

I've always felt as if I see the world in a different way than many people do. I believe it's a gift I've been given. I'm not suggesting I have the power to see into the future or anything like that, but I do believe that seeing the world from a slightly different angle has helped me become who I am and accomplish all that I have.

When others see obstacles, I see opportunities.

When others see failure, I see a chance to learn.

When others see the impossible, I see what could be.

I want to challenge you to see things differently. I want you to see yourself as someone who is uniquely gifted and special. You may not yet fully understand the gift that is within you, but you are—already—very special. Our gifts and talents have been given specifically to us for a reason. Whether you feel special or not, the truth is that you are. Even when you feel out of place and see things differently than everyone else, you are uniquely you. Embrace who you are, and never let anyone intimidate you because they think you're someone different than who you really are inside. We are all different and unique in our own way. We need to learn to appreciate the beautiful differences in one another.

Be you. That's the person I like, even without knowing you. Why? Because you are unique and gifted and probably feel a little out of place, just like I do.

Chapter 10

Wandering Through Life

You have to reach through the dark to find an answer.

After I graduated from high school, I bounced from job to job for a time. It seemed that as soon as I found a job, I found a reason to no longer be employed there. Well, actually, most of the time I got fired. The truth is I didn't like to work, and that was a big problem.

At this point in my life, Milwaukee may have been my hometown, but it became the one place I didn't want to be anymore. I decided to head to Minnesota as a way of starting over. I had some friends up there, and I needed to get away. I had no idea what I was doing with my life, and I had no plan. I just assumed that things would fall into place.

I stayed in Minnesota for just six months. Nothing against the place; I think I just realized how much I missed Milwaukee. I missed my friends. I missed what was familiar to me. I missed my family. There was something within me that made me feel it was time to go home again. I started realizing that everything I left behind was so important to me.

So at twenty, I moved back to Milwaukee. My attitude was completely different from what it was when I had left. I had a much more positive outlook on life. I can't really explain it. When you remove yourself from what is familiar—even for a short period of time—and then return, many things seem new. Things I had taken for granted became things I greatly appreciated. Sometimes our familiarity with things can blind us to their true value.

Finding My Place

When I got back to Milwaukee, I stayed with friends and bounced around from house to house. I would stay as long as they would let me. There would always come a time for *that* conversation: that it was time for me to move along and find another place to live.

It was hard not having a place I could call home. It certainly matched how I felt inside. I was all over the place mentally, emotionally, and spiritually.

The hardest part about moving around so much and being completely dependent on other people is that you begin to lose your sense of self-worth. You begin to see yourself as a burden to others and having no future. I really had to fight against that, but I also didn't know exactly what I was fighting for.

The first weekend after getting back to Milwaukee, I went to a new church called Faith Builders. It was really hip and had great music and a bunch of people my age. I was hungry to be something more than I was. I didn't have all the answers, but I started seeking to become a better person. I wanted to look for the story God has written for my life.

I knew I wanted to be a better me, but I didn't know how to do that. This is really where I started learning what God thought about me, which helped shape my self-image. I started to hang around other people who wanted to be all they were created to be, and this inspired me to do the same. It started to transform my mind. It pushed me to find my place. I didn't realize until then how much influence the people we surround ourselves with have on us. People can either push us toward our best version of ourselves or influence us to be a carbon copy of everyone else. Things were starting to come together for me, more than they ever had in the past.

Within a few months of attending this church, I got involved in the praise and worship team. I knew this was confirmation I was on the right track and things were starting to happen for me.

Way More Than a Job

I went from a warehouse job to a telemarketing job to waiting tables. But something was happening inside of me. The lessons and influence and friends I had at my new church were starting to push me toward my purpose.

One of my favorite jobs during this time was working with inner-city kids at Journey House, a nonprofit organization. I worked with kids from four years old all the way up to eighteen. It was my first steady job, and I had my first office (with an actual door). I was paid $20,000 a year. This kind of work made me feel I was doing something significant.

I was the recreational coordinator for a summer camp program and an after-school program. I could never figure out who needed whom more: Did the kids I worked with need me, or did I need them? I suspect it was a little of both. I played basketball with them, went bowling with them, and became part of their lives. Their stories had a tremendous impact on me.

One time when I was working at the summer program, there was a four-year-old boy whose mom forgot to come pick him up. I ended up taking this boy with me because he was left there for several hours. I picked up Sophia and we took him out to eat, all the while trying to reach his mom. We couldn't get in touch with her or any of his emergency contacts. None of the family members listed were answering their phones. He was basically just forgotten. I couldn't believe this was actually happening. How do you forget a child, especially a four-year-old child? His mom eventually came to pick him up around nine that night. She said she had been working.

Things like this happened all the time. There was so much dysfunction in these kids' lives. I had to learn to look past bad attitudes and see what the real issues were with these kids. There were a lot of disrespectful kids, and every single one was part of a broken home. Some of the parents weren't even grown up themselves, and it was shocking to see how they talked to their children. I can understand why the cycle is repeated with these kids. I saw patterns in these kids' lives that mimicked the generations before them and set them up to repeat the same patterns. I knew they could be changed if someone took the time to help them. I have a strong desire to see people break these patterns to a point of freedom. People can't always see the potential of what they can be. I saw myself breaking out of patterns at this time in my life, and I wanted to help these kids do the same. I was able to assess patterns in others and recognize why people do what they do.

Some people are born with a passion to change the world. I feel as though I were born with a blank slate. Anyone could write on me, and it affected me. I didn't know who I was, but I always trusted that I could do more than what I was presently doing. I realized I didn't have to accept the way things were. Some people say there are born leaders. I turned into a leader.

A lot of kids don't know who they are. They may feel like me—a blank slate—and they don't discover who they really are in life. Anyone with a strong voice can come along and influence them, whether for good or bad. I wanted to become a voice of hope for these kids because there were voices of hope that influenced me. I saw the value of investing in people.

There was a time when I felt as if I had no vision and was not headed in a direction of fulfilling my purpose. I wanted to invest in people like others invested in me.

I quickly realized that this is what I love doing most. I felt like I had found my purpose in life. It was way more than just a job; it was an outlet for me. Though I didn't know it yet, this was a huge time of preparation for my future work at Sophia's Heart. From that experience, I knew I wanted to be involved in this kind of work the rest of my life. I saw it as a way to make a difference.

True happiness is found when we discover the treasure in other people. Nonprofit work is focused—or at least it should be—on people in need. I think this is why I connected with the work so much and consider it to be a great fit. I want to leave my legacy within other people.

I really believe that people—not possessions or positions—are the key to our happiness. Sometimes we fill our lives with stuff and run out of room for people when we really should fill our lives with people and leave little room for stuff.

One person can make a difference, and that person can be me—and you. Even when you feel as though you're wandering through life, there is a great deal of clarity that comes from helping someone else in need.

A Time to Reflect

The church I was attending at the time offered me a paid staff position. It didn't pay a lot, but that didn't matter to me. I was more than thrilled to get to work for this church. My impression upon taking the job was that most of my work would center around praise and worship. I was wrong. Because I was the young guy on staff, I was tasked with all the stuff other people didn't want to do: changing the church sign, mowing the lawn, painting, running wires and cable lines through every single ceiling tile in every single room, and even day care. You get the point. I reasoned that it was okay because I was working for the church. But it became a point of frustration because I wanted to do something I was passionate about and not have to do all the other things I was doing outside of praise and worship. Unfortunately, the church didn't have the budget to justify hiring me as only a music director.

I figured I was working for God, so I was willing to do whatever I was asked to do. We have an uncanny way of telling ourselves stories that seem to smooth out the rough edges of what doesn't seem to be right or fit together seamlessly. Nevertheless, that job kept me deeply involved in the place that allowed me to sing lead onstage, which was — unknown to me at the time — preparing me for something even bigger in my future yet again.

While you're wandering through life, you can't always see the point of why you're doing things. But in hindsight, I can see how all the details were important. God was putting all the pieces together for me, and I had to follow what I knew was true. A lot of people would've given up or quit, but following what I knew in my heart was right allowed me to see the pieces come together.

I decided I didn't want to continue being frustrated about my situation at the church, which paid too little and required too much. My money situation was depressing, but I thought I should keep my job at the church because it was ministry, so I remembered my dad's example and got a second job to make ends meet.

In addition to working at the church, I started driving a truck. I never went to truck-driving school. I purchased a book, taught myself what I needed to know, and took the test. I passed on my first try — by one point. (I think it would've been better if I'd failed; I'm sure I cost this company many dollars.)

With my commercial driver's license in hand, I was hired and paired with an experienced driver to show me the ropes. I learned the hard way how to drive a truck: I damaged a lot of things. I took down stop signs and ruined loads I was shipping because of hitting my brakes too hard, which caused the product to shift and fall into the semitrailer. I once even wrecked an entire semi. I don't recommend skipping driving school. I learned quickly there is a good reason those schools exist. My financial struggles were a burden and stress on me. I was working two jobs, and it affected my performance, I'm sure. To this day, I have no idea why the trucking company kept me.

I had a lot of time to myself while driving and waiting at the loading docks. I started listening to books on tape and radio programs such as The Dave Ramsey Show. I learned I needed to get out of debt and start using money as a way to create opportunity for myself and build my way to a better future. Up until then, I thought I knew it all and had gotten myself into a lot of debt.

This second job allowed me time to listen to the radio and hear a message about money management—a message I needed to hear but wasn't willing to pursue on my own. As I mentioned before, learning about money was invaluable for Sophia and me when we first got married and needed to pay off our debt.

I also continued to read about business and what it meant to be an entrepreneur. I quickly learned I wasn't going to make any real money working for someone else. I was happy to have the jobs I had, but I wanted more.

This is where my drive to understand and practice good business principles was formed—not so I could make a bunch of money and keep it to myself but so I could give a lot of it away. I wanted to stop investing in banks through interest payments. Instead, I wanted to invest in the things that really matter: people.

Let me be clear: I'm not attached to money for money's sake. I have a deep desire to help other people. One of the things I've learned working in the nonprofit space is how limited you can feel by what money is available to resource a vision. You are well aware that the amount of money available to you from donations and grants can limit your ability to help people. It can be a frustrating and discouraging place to be at times.

I've struggled in so many different ways, but my desire and

hunger for something more is one constant in my life. I wanted to be the source of funding for organizations and programs I believed in. That is a part of who I am today.

My time as a truck driver was a turning point for me. No, I didn't suddenly become wealthy or figure out all of life. But I started heading in a new direction: forward. And there is something that happens when you start to move forward with boldness and confidence. What didn't make sense before starts to make sense, and the pieces come together.

Moving forward is a step toward hope because there is more ahead of you than behind you. We know that when the pain comes, the questions flood in, and the threads of life unravel, we just need to hang on. Something new is happening within us, and that something new is the strength we will need to accept the good things that are coming.

If we are not prepared, then our coming prosperity may be wasted.

If we are not positioned, then our coming influence may be misapplied.

If we are not platformed, then our coming leadership may be ineffective.

A Hunger for More

One of the first things I did to move forward after that was stop living with other people. I wanted to find my own place. However, I was not yet in a position financially to afford my own apartment, so I looked for someone who might let me rent out a room.

I ended up renting a guy's walk-in closet for $125 a month as a way to save money. The closet was so small that after putting a twin mattress on the floor and a 3-drawer night stand in there, it was very difficult to shut the door. And because it was a closet, I had clothes hanging over my bed that served as a canopy. I used to see ants on the floor and roaches in our kitchen (and even a mouse in our bathroom once).

It wasn't much, but it was mine. I thought it was great. I lived in that closet for at least six months.

The apartment where I lived in this closet was in the ghetto, and I stuck out big-time. Living in the hood means you learn to live with a sense of the unknown. You have to pay attention to every noise because something is always happening — usually something bad.

One night I was walking from the alley into my apartment and I heard the faint sound of footsteps. I turned around and saw a huge half-naked man. Then all of a sudden, two other half-naked guys popped out from behind a car. I looked at them and told them they have the wrong guy and quickly unlocked the door to my apartment. I managed to wiggle out of the situation without harm. Things like this happened at random all the time in this neighborhood.

I also learned what to do during a drive-by shooting. In the ghetto, a drive-by is strangely normal. When you hear the *pow-pow-pow* of the guns going off, you know what's happening. A reasonable person hits the ground. The first time I saw a drive-by, I noticed an SUV blocks down the street slow down in front of a house. I then heard the guns go off, and the SUV drove away. Everyone around me dropped to the ground. It took me a few minutes to realize what had just happened. I decided it would be a good idea to follow their lead and drop down when I heard gunshots next time.

When it comes to crime, winters weren't as bad as summers. I think the cold sent everyone into hibernation mode. But once spring hit, things got crazy. It's like all the anger built up over the winter was let loose all at once when the weather got warm again.

This part of my life gave me great compassion for people who feel stuck and unable to move forward. I found myself wanting to help myself so I could eventually help others move toward hope too.

Adventures Unfolding with Every Step

The dark times of our lives are when we have little certainty about what will come next. Those times can clarify our intentions or confuse our sense of direction. There is no escaping the moments when we simply have to reach forward and hope that there is something to grab hold of before we begin to lose our balance and fall away.

The moments and experiences you think life is using to break you are the exact moments you are being prepared for something even bigger. It is our:

Pain that leads to joy.

Questions that lead to wisdom.

Patience that leads to unshakable faith.

Endurance that leads to our victory.

Looking forward can be difficult; moving forward is even harder. Nothing seems to be connected. Few things make sense. It isn't until we are on the other side of our struggle that we begin to see how connected our struggle is to our success.

Life is a series of course corrections. Sometimes the road is dark, and that can be discouraging. Who would have guessed the twists and turns in my life? These are things only God can know, but they are the adventures that unfold with every step. The key is to keep moving forward until you find the answer, desire, or confidence you need and trust that you are not alone.

It is always most difficult to move through those times in life when nothing adds up and you feel as though you're moving backward. You are restless inside, and there are few things you can count on. You desperately want a road map or something to tell you what to do next. But even if that existed for me in my dark times, I probably wouldn't have used it. This is what makes faith and hope so important. It allows us to focus on the endgame and our dreams. If we focus on those things when we're going through dark times, life won't seem as bad because we know there are better days ahead.

Sometimes the only way through the dark is to wait for the

dawn. You have to reach through the dark to find hope and an answer. If you have the courage to endure, you'll begin to see your next steps unfold before your very eyes.

Chapter 11

Strength from Within

Don't miss out on the good things right in front of you.

People want something they can worship. Some people want to *be* worshipped. And they are willing to do whatever it takes to get it, even if it means losing themselves in the process.

The road of life can be a long and lonely one. People want to know there is more to life—at least for someone else if they are not strong enough to believe it for themselves. We must believe that life is more than right now.

American Idol gives people—most you don't know and have never heard of—a chance to take the world's stage and become someone who is larger than life. The magic of the show is in watching a celebrity be born right before your eyes. It really is a remarkable experience whether you are the person on the platform, in the audience, or watching from home.

The show was the first of its kind in a long time. It reinvigorated a generation around a music-themed show. This had not been done since Star Search in the 1980s. There were other similar shows, but it had been a long time since a music-based contest had captured the hearts and minds of a mainstream audience.

A Far-Fetched Idea

All my hopes for a career in music had been fading, had been put on hold, and seemed far-fetched. Sophia and I had talked a lot about my love for music and my dream to make music my full-time work. We even discussed pursuing the most unlikely of starts: through the television show *American Idol.*

Sophia loved the show from its first season. She watched it religiously. I really wasn't that interested in it for a long time. That is, until season 7. That's when I started watching the show and Sophia and I started talking about the possibility of my trying out for season 8.

Initially, I didn't take it very seriously. I was working so much, and it seemed unlikely that I would be able to stop my life to compete on the show. But the more I watched, the more excited I got about it. I even went to my pastor, whose opinion meant so much to me, to get his advice and blessing. He gave them, neither of us knowing at the time what dramatic changes were in store for me.

Having a music career was certainly a goal of mine. With each passing year, I felt that it was becoming more and more difficult to get noticed and have any chance at the career I wanted. I certainly wasn't content with where things were at the time, but I wondered if there was any chance at making it.

Sophia and I decided I would give it a shot and try to make the season 8 show. We knew the cutoff age was twenty-eight and that would be the last year I could try out. I believed that was the end of the line for my dream. If I couldn't make it on the show, a music career was probably impossible.

It still seemed too crazy to give it much consideration, but I wanted to make a run of it and see what happened. I felt as though I had been preparing for this for years, and this just might be my big chance. But then Sophia's health deteriorated.

The initial audition was on August 8, 2008 — one month after I'd lost Sophia. I had picked that date for auditions months before Sophia's surgery.

I was broken and not in a good place. I was crying and in such turmoil. In fact, I didn't want to try out. This was not how I wanted to present myself to a national audience. But I knew how excited Sophia had been about it, and I knew she would have wanted me to try out. I tried to keep it together as best as I could, but I was hurting deeply inside. I wanted time to grieve and recover but knew I didn't have another year because of the cutoff age, and I promised Sophia I would try.

Then it occurred to me that maybe something good could come out of this and maybe God has a purpose for me in all of this. That suddenly brought me a ray of hope for the first time since Sophia's death. It didn't take the pain away immediately, but the healing process begins when you have hope. Focusing my eyes on the hope of the show took my eyes off the hopeless loss I just went through and put things in better perspective.

Change Ahead

Most people don't understand there are four rounds of auditions that take place before anyone gets to Hollywood. They know only what they see on TV. The first round of auditions was in Kansas City, Missouri. I was still living in Milwaukee at the time, and it was about an eight-hour drive to Kansas City.

As I stood in line to begin what would ultimately be a twelve-hour day of waiting, I wondered what I was doing there. There were so many people, and we all wanted the same thing. People were doing all sorts of crazy things just to get on camera. I was just trying to keep it together.

The thing I kept wondering to myself was how I was supposed

to stand out in a crowd like this. What made me different from anyone else? It's so easy to get focused on other people and other things and forget what makes you uniquely you.

I battled with myself over whether or not I should even be there, but I remembered my promise to Sophia and that my time was running out. If I didn't take the chance now, it would be too late to honor that promise. Throughout the day, I was in tears one minute and laughing the next. I'm sure people wondered if there was something wrong with me.

I'm so grateful my friends Jamar, Sophia's cousin Marilyn, and Marilyn's husband, Pito, were with me on this journey. I'm not sure I would have made it through the day without them. They helped remind me I wasn't alone.

The first round of auditions is called the "cattle call." They call it that because they herded more than ten thousand of us into the dome. We sat in the arena for what seemed like forever. Then they called one section at a time to the center of the auditorium, where they had twelve booths side by side, separated by curtains. We lined up in rows of four and one by one took a step forward to sing about twenty to thirty seconds of a song.

The audition experience was overwhelming. The sea of people who had the same dream I did, the endless posturing before my competition, and the repetitive auditions in front of various groups of producers made the whole experience feel much more like a chaotic circus than an artful performance. This was my only shot, and I desperately needed something good to happen.

Out of ten thousand people, I was one of about five hundred given the chance to come back in October and audition again.

When I got the callback, I should have been ecstatic. And I was, in a lot of ways. But I was also dealing with tremendous inner turmoil. The vision of Sophia being lowered into her grave haunted me. I wanted to grab hold of her. I wanted to breathe life into her again. I wanted anything but the fate I had been dealt, even the one that included this callback. I was living a perfect paradox. The possibility of realizing my dream was never more real, yet my soul felt heavy, broken, and fractured.

Losing My Grip

After my first audition, I was really in a bad place emotionally. There were several more auditions ahead and a few months before the show actually started taping, so there were no guarantees I would keep moving forward in the process, although things seemed to be headed that way. I was supposed to be excited, but the pain kept growing. Sophia meant the world to me—way more than the show ever did or could. I just wanted my wife back. My depression had fully set in. I tried my best to pull it all together because I was doing this for Sophia. My experience was very different from that of the other contestants. The highs and lows were amplified. I couldn't appreciate the fullness of the moment because I was numb inside. I often walked around oblivious to anything or anyone else because I was lost in my own thoughts.

I was mad and frustrated. I had done all the right things. I'd prayed all the right prayers. We'd gone to the doctors, followed their instructions, and were religious about any treatment plan or regimen they suggested. Still, Sophia died.

I could tell I was losing my grip on life. The initial audition process was successful, and initially I was happy. But once the high went away, the pain crept back in. I don't know if you've ever been there, but I was hurting so much inside I couldn't even think straight. I could no longer see hope.

I thought making it through the first audition meant God was working something out for me. But then I started doubting what I believed. I thought I was crazy for having hope. My emotions started poisoning my heart, and I could no longer see the beauty of where I was and the great things that were just ahead.

The moment I started doubting my faith and hope and asking myself where the proof was, everything changed: Things got worse.

I woke up one morning in September and felt something change. It was like I could sense a shift in the atmosphere in my room, and I knew it wasn't good. I had been trying to stay positive up to this point and ignore the growing pain inside. That day when I woke up, my emotions had taken over, which is never good. Feelings are fickle, and they can take you down a bad road if you let them. Once I took my eyes off the good things that were happening to me, I literally felt like I was falling, and I couldn't get back up. It was like the floor dropped out from under me and I couldn't catch the walls. When the floor drops out from under you, no answer is good enough.

I hated living. I felt I was stupid to believe that something good would be coming. Nothing good had happened in my past. I had already experienced the worst, so why should I believe? In the days that followed, I'd wake up in the morning and wish I could go back to sleep again. But when I was sleeping, I wanted to be awake because of the nightmares I was having. It was a horrible place to be.

I tried to sleep a lot because sleep was my only escape, but I couldn't sleep most nights. I was full of anxiety. My heart was beating really fast, and I didn't have an appetite. It affected everything. It even affected my breathing.

When you fall into that pit and don't focus on the good, your life seems worse than it is. Even though my situation was not the worst in the world, and there are way worse situations than what I've been through, I was sucked into a despair that magnified my problems. I became so self-absorbed that I felt as though I had the worst life in the world. I didn't put my situation into proper perspective. I blew it up so far beyond its proportions. I lived in a false reality, and it was the worst place to live. I hated every moment of it, and I despised living. I was consumed with how I felt, but in some ways it was self-inflicted because I couldn't change my focus. I had unrealistic expectations to the point that I started making demands of

God. I remember telling Him to send a real angel from heaven and a parting of the skies to show me that hope is real—or it's just not real.

When our hearts are poisoned, our outlooks on life are poisoned. I later realized the key to letting go meant being okay with not having the answer. I was falling only because I doubted what I did have. The deep depression came when I lost sight of hope. It felt as though I had no reason to live. I was angry at God, yet I knew down deep inside that He was the only one who had the answer and without Him there was no hope for me.

My heart had been tainted. When I finally was able to rid myself of the bitterness, I started seeing *American Idol* as a beautiful opportunity. Suddenly *everything* seemed more beautiful to me.

I never want to look back on my life and wish I had taken that chance or rolled the dice on an opportunity. I want to know I took every opportunity, every chance, and never let a moment slip by because I was held captive by fear, doubt, and uncertainty. It's an exciting and risky way to live, for sure. It takes courage to live without regrets.

One of the Best

I had to go back to Kansas City on October 15, 2008, for my next audition. Instead of thousands of people, there were only about five hundred people this time. I would have to go through two more rounds of auditions that day in order to earn the right to audition before the judges. From the thousands of people who show up to the first audition, less than fifty in each city get to actually audition before the television judges (another little-known fact for those who watch the show).

I walked into the room to my first audition around 2:00 p.m. Before me was a panel of producers, coaches, and show staff. It was very intimidating. I sang a Brian McKnight song, only to have them request I sing something else. Then it was finally my time to audition in front of the show judges. I had made it to the make or break audition.

I walked into the audition room. My whole body was numb, and I was nervous. These are the people who will ultimately decide your fate—the people you want to affirm and approve you to move forward.

For this audition, I sang "I Heard It Through the Grapevine." To my surprise, they loved it. Randy even commented that I was one of the best they'd heard all day. Wow! What a compliment!

When you have no hope, you'll cling to anything, so to hear the reviews they gave me sparked me. I grabbed on to that hope.

I made it to the next round: Hollywood. It was a surreal experience. I'm not even sure I was taking it all in, which was clearly evident in what happened next.

I had watched the season before, and I always saw contestants walk out of the room in the wrong direction. I told myself that when I tried out, I would not be *that* guy. But after giving all the judges knuckle punches, I walked out of the room the wrong way. Yep, in spite of my best efforts, I became that guy. The judges said in unison, "Wrong way!" It was humiliating, but I was so shocked that I wasn't even thinking straight. Yet I didn't even care: I had hope.

I still remember the feeling of walking out of the room with that yellow sheet of paper. It felt amazing. Ryan Seacrest and my family and friends were waiting, and the celebration began. It was a long road, but I had made it. I knew in that moment that Sophia was smiling down on me and was proud of me. I really wished she was there too.

This Has to Work

The show doesn't cover your expenses until you make it to Hollywood. At this point, I had no job and no income. Yet I had to self-fund my way through the audition process and also pay for gas, groceries, and other expenses. Thankfully, we had a little savings, and some very generous people had given me money at Sophia's funeral. It wasn't an amount that would last forever, but I made it stretch. *American Idol* had to work, or I was going to have to make some drastic changes in my life.

Once I finally made it to Hollywood, in addition to my expenses being covered, I received four hundred dollars per show for my wardrobe. For someone who usually shopped at Rue21, where everything is less than ten dollars, the wardrobe allowance seemed like an unbelievable amount of money for clothes—until I started shopping with my stylist. There isn't much you can buy on Melrose Avenue for four hundred dollars. I was in shock when I saw single items of clothing selling for thousands of dollars. I asked my stylist if we could shop in a cheaper part of town, and he immediately shut down that idea. He said his reputation was on the line and I needed to look good for the show. I'm glad he knew what he was doing, or at least *I* thought he did.

Though our stylists were supposed to guide us, we had to make the ultimate decisions. Looking back at the show footage, I can't believe that my stylist allowed me to make some of the choices I did. I wish he had stopped me in some cases. At the time, I thought I was stylish, so I didn't know I needed to be embarrassed. I describe my style now as geek chic, but the chic part definitely came later. On the show, it was mostly geek.

Driven Inside

If there is one thing that kept me from getting tangled in what others thought about me, it's that I was an emotional mess most of the show. I worked through my emotions over time and became very in tune with who I was and who I was created to be. I knew I was not being motivated or driven by the approval of others. Instead, there was something within me that was the source of my strength and resolve to continue to pursue my dream.

You will likely need the same strength to keep pushing through the ups and downs as you pursue your deepest dreams. When your strength comes from within, you will be able to resist the temptation to live out of what others expect of you and live a legacy that will be remembered for many years to come.

If we build our own kingdoms, we will fall when our kingdom falls. If we invest in people, then we will create a legacy that lives forever. I hope your desire to find purpose in your darkest moments drives you inside. There you will find what you need to endure and thrive as you move through life.

My hope was never in *American Idol*. That is just a TV show. My goal has never been to achieve fame but rather to become someone who would be considered great—a man of character, conviction, and resolve. Yet the show did give me something to be excited about and hope for. This hope is the same hope you have for your own dreams, prayers, and goals.

You dream dreams that one day will come true.

You pray prayers that one day will be answered.

You take action today that one day will result in achieving your goals.

Keep pushing forward. The excitement that comes when good things start to unfold is worth it. This was the first time in my life when I felt that my dream of a music career was within reach. It is a refreshing feeling when you're used to working two low-paying jobs and working six days a week with little chance or opportunity for significant change.

Seeing all the chaos around me during the auditions initially made me regret coming, and I felt like I had sold myself out. But it was really because I felt insecure. I thought I might not have what the industry was looking for. I'm so glad I didn't allow those thoughts and lies to consume me. Had I given up and gone home, I would have forfeited the biggest successes that were still ahead for me. Your story has already been written. It's up to you to live out the plan and purpose that's been given to you.

I realize now I could've missed it all if I hadn't dealt with my negative emotions. You have to ask yourself what you're looking at, because what you're looking at becomes you. Right now a lot of people are missing the good things right in front of them. They have sight but can't really see because they've been poisoned like I was during my depression. When I let my depression take over, I didn't even want to be on the show because I allowed my thoughts to poison my heart and thinking. In my mind, the show was a place where I was going to make a fool of myself. I thought God didn't care and I was going to fail miserably.

An opportunity through the lens of bitterness and anger doesn't look like much of an opportunity. I could've missed my opportunity on the show if I wasn't able to change my focus and detox my mind of all the negative thoughts.

There is hope all around us all the time, but if we don't have a pure heart and pure focus, we won't see that hope. Focusing on bad things can ruin a perfectly good thing. I've learned this lesson: When you've prayed and it looks as if God is not doing anything, that's usually when He's working the most. Trust Him. He's got you. When we turn our focus to negative things or feelings, we won't be able to see good even when it comes our way. Good is all around you; make sure you don't miss it.

Chapter 12

Impossibly Me

You are strong enough to keep being you.

When we are children, we easily react when we are hungry, thirsty, and tired. As we get older, we learn to ignore some of our needs and desires until we don't even recognize them within us. It is at this point that we stop living our lives and begin living to the cadence set by those who have convinced us they know us better than ourselves. The tragedy is they may be right.

When you get to Hollywood, there is no more joking. Every singer there is good. You don't get that far on a show like *American Idol* and not have talent and skill. This is where the real competition begins.

My nerves were running high, and I barely slept. I probably logged about two to three hours of sleep every night. It was tough, but I knew that everything was on the line.

At first I thought the competition was with the other contestants on the show. Not true. What I quickly learned is that the real competition is with yourself. Each week you have to out-perform the week before. When you have a great week, you celebrate for a moment. But you quickly realize that you just raised the bar for yourself. If you can't raise it again, you risk people getting bored with you and being unimpressed. That is a risk I knew existed but rarely allowed myself to focus on very long.

Look Beyond What You See

Even though I earned my spot in the Hollywood auditions in October, it wasn't until January that the show actually began. During that time, two significant things happened. I accepted the fact that I had to let go of Sophia. It was hard, and it hurt so much. But as I mentioned before, I couldn't move forward unless I let go of my pain. The second significant event was the formal establishment of Sophia's Heart.

I was starting to heal, but I had a long way to go. Because I was still hurting inside, I kept to myself when I got to Hollywood. I'm sure other contestants thought I was just posturing to throw them off their game. That wasn't the case. If anything, I was fully aware of the talent in the room and felt nervous that I didn't have the emotional resolve to press through.

Most people saw the happy me. They never saw the pain. I was in a mourning process, and I had walls up. While I did my best to hide it, I'm sure the only one I was fooling was myself.

What I wasn't aware of at the time was that this was a divine moment for me. I was being positioned to move into a platform with greater influence. This moment in my life was a game changer. Yet I felt very insignificant and unsure of myself. Nevertheless, I had a sense that something bigger was taking place. I was there not just to sing but to win, and that is exactly what I intended to do.

You learn a lot about yourself when you are around people who are nothing like you. I never realized just how insulated I was from the world. Just as my eyes were opened when I moved from private school to public school growing up, my eyes were again opened on the show to how entrenched I was in the culture of the church.

Church is a culture. That's not a bad thing in and of itself. It has its own language, customs, expectations, and assumptions. I love church, so please don't think I am knocking the church in any way. But the gap is evident when you get around people who aren't part of a church.

It is surprising to me that when the word *God* is used, people quickly react in a very negative way. It's okay to talk about anything else, but when you start talking about your faith, some people react very negatively and refuse to engage in the dialogue.

Unintentionally, I probably came off as being self-righteous. I recognized just how judgmental I could be. I don't mean that I looked down on people. On the contrary. I've never considered myself as perfect, nor did I expect anyone else to be. When I say judgmental, I mean having preconceived ideas about choices people make. I quickly learned that I never have the whole story until I hear the story from the person directly.

The same is true for the homeless people I worked with through the church and whom we serve through Sophia's Heart. It's easy to look at a homeless person and think they could do better for themselves if they would just take responsibility for their lives and get a job. But I've learned it is rarely that simple. They have addictions, emotional pain, and a variety of other things that keep them from making good choices. They need help, just like we all do at times.

A Lingering Sense of Failure

Once I finally made the show, I was faced with the challenge of choosing a new song to perform each week. This is another area where my church background really came into play. I knew mostly church and gospel songs, so when I would get the list of songs to choose from, I felt as if I were already at a huge disadvantage. I had no idea which song was the right one to choose, let alone how to select one that "fit" me. It felt like an impossible task.

Part of the expectation on the show was singing and performing, but you also wanted to put your own spin on the song you chose to perform. I didn't know the song to begin with. That meant I had to learn the song first and then find a way to make it my own. That's fine if you are in a studio with plenty of time; that's not fine if you have only a few days to learn, arrange, and perform.

When it came time to go on the show, I was taken over by nerves. The pressure was overwhelming, and I was afraid I'd forget the words to the song I was supposed to perform that night. I'd recite the words to myself over and over again. Still, when Ryan Seacrest would welcome the TV audience back to the show and announce my name, my mind would go blank for a moment. Then, like a tape feeding through a machine, the words always came back to me.

I never forgot the words on the show. I'm grateful for that. But there were times when the music would start, and I was still grasping for the first line or two of the song. Once I got the first word out, the rest just flowed.

Everything was happening so fast. I couldn't make sense of life or process all that was happening around me as part of my experience on the show. That fear never completely went away. When you are under that much pressure, you constantly wrestle with the high potential for failure. I lived with the nagging thought that someone might figure out just how much of an emotional mess I was at the time. I was grateful each week when I was given one more chance to be able to do it again the coming week.

I didn't know what I was more grateful for: the fact that I survived another week or the fact that I was able to avoid dealing with what life would look like if this didn't work out the way I hoped it might. I remember thinking to myself that if this didn't work out, I didn't know what I was going to do next.

That's a hard way to live. Maybe you're not living a life that is on the stage with millions of viewers on the other end of the camera waiting for you to fail or succeed. Maybe you'd never even be on a show like *American Idol.* That doesn't matter. Living with a sense of failure is something that haunts all of us at some point and in some way.

It can become easy to give in to the expectations of others, especially those you perceive to be better than you in some way. Just remember that not everyone who appears to be living a perfect life really is. Whatever advice or correction you are given should not be assumed to be without flaw. Be careful which people you allow the honor of influencing your decisions and shaping your life.

The challenge is not to allow fear to chase you into submitting to others' expectations. Instead, let fear activate the desires of your heart and the dreams of your spirit to see that hope is real. That is when failure is transformed into opportunity, defeat is transformed into victory, and dead ends become the next steps in discovering your purpose.

More Than Music

There is no doubt the judges make the show much of what it is. They are certainly who they are in real life. What you see on TV is accurate. Those are their personalities. But all of them absolutely understand what it takes to make good TV.

After seeing them on TV the previous season, I thought they looked smaller when I saw them in person. It was just different. TV makes everyone look bigger than they are in real life. I don't mean bigger in size; I mean larger than life. I'm talking more about perception than science.

We used to joke that Simon was the father (or the godfather), Paula was the mom, and Randy was the big brother. You wanted all of them to like you, but each of them spoke into your experience in a unique and specific way. Still, seeing them behind the table at the audition and later after every performance was daunting and overwhelming. You were never quite sure how they were going to react. You always hoped they liked what you did, but you could never know for sure.

I get asked a lot if I had personal interaction with the judges like the contestants do on *The Voice* and *The X Factor*, where the judges directly mentor the contestants. For the most part, we saw the judges only when the audience did on performance nights. Don't get me wrong: They gave us input, but we didn't have a lot of direct interaction with them.

In addition, they may call it the music business, but I can assure you there is not an equal preference given to music and business. The show is about music, singing, and performing, yet I did less of that than anything else while on the show. That was shocking to me.

There were photo shoots, sponsor appearances, special events, TV and radio spots, and many other obligations that filled our schedules. It was a huge learning curve for me and something not everyone fully understands or gets to experience by just watching.

American Idol is a success on two fronts: It helps discover new talent, and it creates such a buzz that it is able to command top dollar for advertising spots, sponsorships, and similar revenue-generating endeavors. I'm not saying that I don't respect the business part in the music business. It was just something new for me, and I had to learn to get used to it and adjust. The strange thing is that it quickly becomes normal and you stop questioning, wondering, and being surprised.

A Beautiful Song

The pressure was coming down harder and harder as the weeks went by. The fewer the contestants, the brighter the spotlight. People love cheering for the underdog, and I held that position until the end.

Still, I had to intentionally separate myself each week from the reality that this could be my last week. I knew I couldn't win if I focused on staying another week. That's no way to win a competition because it doesn't allow you to take risks. You can't hold back when you are competing on a show like *American Idol*.

I knew that my only chance of winning was to pour myself out on the stage, and that's what I did. Some of my best performances were "PYT (Pretty Young Thing)," "Come Rain or Shine," and "You Are So Beautiful." My lowest weeks were the ones when I gave in to the pressure and started thinking about the people on the other end of the camera and the judges behind the table.

In addition, getting to sing with Lionel Richie and be mentored by Randy Travis was amazing. In fact, it was Randy Travis who encouraged me to pursue country music once the show was over. He said he was of the opinion that country music could use some more soul.

In the midst of it all, I learned that it was okay to be me, even if I was a mess inside. I knew who I was. There is a strange freedom that comes from living with an extreme amount of pain. We forget about all the expectations we've internalized from others. We lose the ability to keep track of what others say, think, and believe about us.

They tell you when you make the show not to look at what people are saying about you online and to avoid any feedback and commentary from anyone other than yourself, the judges, voice coaches, and show producers. But of course you can't help but look. I quickly learned what they meant. Whoever said all press is good press has never had their wife's death used against them, their words twisted, and their intentions questioned. It never occurred to me that my story could be used against me.

I came across a cartoon-like drawing that was supposed to be me dragging Sophia out of her casket and a caption that read, "Danny, stop capitalizing on my death to make yourself famous. Let me rest in peace." That was tough to read and see. The person who posted this drawing argued that I was wrongfully using my loss of Sophia to win the show. Nothing could be further from the truth. The pain I felt inside was too real for it to be some ploy to gang the system and win.

I quickly realized I couldn't focus on negative things because it was affecting me. I started having nightmares and woke up crying at night. Had I been focused on things that were encouraging and uplifting, I wouldn't have struggled, but I was focusing on something that really got me off track. It affected my thinking, and I had to take my eyes off that negativity. It affected my sleep patterns and my performance. I learned very quickly that the power of what we focus on really does affect our thinking and even our health. It was destroying me, and I literally felt sick. When you're looking at the wrong things and not focused on hope, it affects you.

No matter where you are in life, you will be pulled in a lot of different directions. You will be presented with a lot of different ideas. You will be expected to be, say, and do a lot of different things. Never forget to stay true to what you know is true, even if it seems impossible. It's so easy to get lost in the noise and forget that hope contains the rhythm that turns notes into melodies, words into lyrics, and arrangements into masterpieces. Your life is a beautiful song. If you are brave enough to sing it in your way, you will discover a hope that will carry you, and those around you will be challenged to do the same.

While I was on the show, I got lots of e-mails and letters from people who were going through struggles. There was a woman in particular whose boyfriend had committed suicide a few months before, and she too was contemplating taking her own life. On the night she was contemplating suicide, she heard me crying on TV and walked up to the TV and heard my story. She found so much hope in my story that she decided not to do it.

You have greater influence on others than you may realize or think. There may be people depending on you to make it, and you may not even realize it right now. Sometimes what you're going through is bigger than you. You could be someone else's hope and strength to make it through another day.

Imagine if I would have caved in to the dark thoughts during my depression. I'd have missed the opportunity to help so many people, especially now at Sophia's Heart. But because I had hope, I was able to give hope to others as well.

Sometimes we need to look at the bigger picture. What if what you're going through has nothing to do with you and it's for someone else? There is a domino effect. If you cling to hope and make it through, you're going to be strength for someone else. You're going to be hope for others who think they can't make it. You never know who you can inspire. What if you are the person who will give hope to someone who will start the next rehab center for thousands of drug addicts? It may be unseen to you while you're in the middle of something tough, but your life is something bigger and means more than just what you're going through now.

My End Was a Beginning

Most people think being voted off a show like *American Idol* would be disappointing. For me, while I certainly wanted to win, when my time came to an end, it was a release of all the pressure and somewhat of a relief. But I was also proud of myself. Ten months before, I stood at my wife's casket and wanted to die along with her. And now I was in the top three, and I had never been in the bottom three. Eighty-eight million people voted for that results show. It was an accomplishment even though I didn't win.

Simon Cowell gave me some great advice. He said, "Don't worry about genre; just make good music. Good music sells." That wisdom has stuck with me to this day and is some of the best career advice I've ever received.

During my exit interview as I was leaving the show, I said that I saw my music as a movement. I'm sure this sounded crazy. I could see it in my mind, but I admit I had no idea exactly how it would take shape. But after saying that, I started working toward that.

When I left the show, I had a purpose that kept me going. I had the promise of a music career because I had made it so far on the show, but I also had a developing vision for Sophia's Heart. The motivation to honor Sophia's memory was still fresh and strong, which forged a determination in me to make something happen.

During the show, someone offered to donate two thousand dollars to each of the top ten contestants' charities of choice. Even though the vision wasn't fully formed and Sophia's Heart only existed on paper at that point, both Kris Allen and Michael Sarver believed in it enough to choose Sophia's Heart as their beneficiary. I was honored. They saw something in it before the vision had even been expanded on.

Strong Enough to Be You

Life can be overwhelming. The temptation is real to start looking for approval from others. In my case, I could have easily hinged my entire self-worth on the judge's decision and what other people thought of me, but I didn't. I was so messed up that all I could think about was doing a good job for Sophia, which—ironically—may have saved me from falling into that trap. Nevertheless, it is easy to redirect our attention to other people and look for affirmation from external sources.

Instead, you should look within. You must recognize that you are a beautiful person. You are uniquely gifted. That's why it's important to get comfortable in your own skin.

You are smart enough.

You are good-looking enough.

You are talented enough.

You have the capacity to be and accomplish whatever exists within the depths of your heart. You can make it. I know it's possible, because I have lived it.

I had a unique set of judges who decided whether or not I would make it on the show. But everyone is faced with a group of judges who we think determine our fate. That simply isn't true. No one decides your fate but you. If you don't voice what you know to be true, others will make you who they think you are. This is why it's so important that you find the strength to be you. Don't try to be someone else. Don't try to be perfect. Don't try to live up to the expectations of other people. Instead, start living from a place within you that represents the truth and beauty of who you are and who you were created to be.

You are strong enough to keep being you. Follow your heart and the hope you have. Pay attention to those people and experiences that make your heart skip a beat inside. Those are insights into who you are and who you are becoming.

Even if you have denied who you are up to this point, you don't have to continue in that same direction. Live in your own lane. And don't use your turn signal until you know that the desire to switch lanes is coming from the hope and truth of who you really are that resides within *you*. That's when you find true freedom. It will give you a whole new sense of feeling alive. In fact, being who you were created to be—and celebrating that—is the only life worth living.

Before you can love with your whole heart, it must be yours to give away.

Before you can live with reckless abandon, it must be yours to live.

Before you can have faith, it must be yours to possess.

What is before us is greater than what is behind us. The divine gift of hope you've been given has been specifically crafted with you in mind. When you are strong enough to be you and keep being you, you'll find what you've been looking for.

You are a divine gift to the world. You were created with unique talents and abilities that afford you the ability to do things not everyone can do. That doesn't mean you have to sing onstage, reside on a bookshelf, or paint on a canvas. In fact, the greatest gift you can give someone else will never be able to be captured through concerts, books, or paintings. The gift is love.

We were created to have relationships with people. But too often we exchange the purity of connecting with another human being for the expectations of culture: to live in front of a screen, drive in the fast lane, and get while the getting is good.

What good is achieving success or living out others' expectations of us if we lose ourselves in the process? I would rather stay true to my own voice and follow the desires of my heart and skip success than give all my uniqueness away and live by an expectation defined by someone else. I want to live a little more dangerously. I don't just want a career in music; I want to use music to inspire people to break free from whatever is holding them back from lunging toward their divine destiny.

You already have everything you need to be a stunning success. It's okay to listen to the advice of people who are farther down the path than you are and have been where you are, but never exchange the desires of your heart for anything this world has to offer. The strength of your hope depends on your ability to reach forward in a direction no one has likely gone before or at least in the way you will. The gift is you, so don't try to be anyone else.

Chapter 13

A Greater Plan

You have to hope there's something better coming or you won't move toward it.

Forward motion creates momentum. Having something to live for and look forward to can give us the energy we need to pull us through our questions and doubt. It is the single-greatest catalyst we can experience to create personal change.

American Idol positioned me on a platform I likely never would've had access to outside the show. With that platform, momentum started building and things began to take off. Even though I didn't end up winning, landing in the top three secured the public interest I needed to attract the attention of the industry. In other words, the show put me in front of the right people—the people who had the power to sign me to a record label.

When you make *American Idol*, you are signed to the record label 19 Records. Once the show was finished, Sony Music had the option to sign me or release me to talk to other labels. Sony exercised their right to sign me, and I was assigned to Sony Music in

Nashville. I was fortunate to leave the show with a deal in hand, as that wasn't the case for everyone.

Immediately after the show, we began practicing for the *American Idol* tour, which began in June. The pressure was off, the show was over, and now it was time to have some fun. We got to learn what it was like to live on the road. Going from city to city as quickly as we did was exhausting and exhilarating at the same time. I went from one of the world's largest stages to having a record contract and being on tour. Things were really looking up.

Once the tour ended, the real work began. With my label in Nashville, it only made sense that I should be in Nashville too. I had moved away from Milwaukee once before, but back then I was running away from things I didn't know how to deal with. I was restless and just needed to get away and change my environment.

This move wasn't anything like that. I was in a different place in my life now. Nashville started to seem like the best option, considering all the new and different things emerging in my life. I felt as though this time I was running *toward* something.

It seemed like the best decision, so I decided to make the move. I was sorry to leave behind my hometown. I will always be a Milwaukee native, and I will cheer for only the Green Bay Packers. I was just going to have to do that from Nashville now.

Gaining Momentum

Immediately, the next phase of my career started ramping up. I had meetings with record executives and started planning out the next phases of my career, which included award shows and television appearances to gain exposure before my first album released. I was sitting with writers, picking songs, and spending time in the studio right away. I had the opportunity to work with amazing studio musicians who have worked with the best in the industry.

The opportunities I had hoped for and prayed about for years were finally playing out before my eyes. It was surreal. Having my own tour bus right after the show was something I had only dreamed about. It's a small thing, but to me that was a sign of success. Suddenly people recognized me on the street. Fans actually wanted to buy tickets to see me at my own shows. It was time to seize the opportunity and ride the wave.

Being fresh off the show, you get all kinds of people wanting to help you capitalize on your success. For me, part of what stood out to people on *American Idol* (besides my voice, hopefully) was my glasses. I made it a point to wear different glasses each week as a distinguishing factor. Naturally, my glasses caught the attention of some vendors, and I received offers to endorse products or create a line. One offer stood out to me as a hometown boy from Wisconsin. A multistate vision store chain based in Milwaukee saw me on the show and asked me to be a spokesperson for their stores. As a result of that connection, their manufacturer, Match Eyewear, caught the vision of a bigger picture and chose to leverage my exposure on the show to create the Danny Gokey Eyewear Collection.

Although there were other offers and endorsement deals that came my way, this one was really a cool thing for me. To think that one of the things that made me unique (actually, one of the things I was teased about as a kid) was now shaping a part of my future. Life had certainly taken a turn in the most incredible ways.

My first album, "My Best Days," released in 2010 and garnered first-week album sales that were the best of any debut male country artist in eighteen years. I couldn't believe it. We sold 65,000 records the first week. It also earned a number one position in chart history with the best first-week digital-album sales ever recorded by a debut country act to that point and reached number four on the weekly Billboard 200 album chart.

My first single release was "My Best Days Are Ahead of Me." That was a special song for me—an anthem of sorts. I originally picked the song because it represented my future and everything I had overcome up until that point. The song was pitched to us and we picked it for the album having never talked to the author who penned it. It wasn't until later that it came to mean even more to me once I met the songwriter, Kent Blazy.

Kent has written some amazing hits, such as "If Tomorrow Never Comes," which Garth Brooks recorded. Just like I faced the reality of having to find the strength to move forward without Sophia, Kent had to say good-bye to his wife, Sharon, after twenty-eight years of marriage. They had fought her brain tumors for a long time. One day she decided she was tired of fighting the inevitable. She was going to die, and trying to postpone it wasn't going to change that. The only way Kent could process what he was feeling was to do what he had been divinely gifted to do: write songs.

Kent's pain had to be great. He had spent almost three decades with the love of his life. I felt like my heart was ripped out of my chest and my life was completely off course after only four years of marriage. I couldn't imagine being twenty-eight years into it and having to say good-bye.

Yet in the midst of the pain, Kent wrote the lyrics to a song about the promise of a better tomorrow. Kent shared his very personal song with his friend Marv Green. Together they polished Kent's pain into a song of hope and promise of what is to come. Little did Kent or Marv know I would later record that song having dealt with the same pain.

I didn't just sing that song; I lived it and believed it. I felt like only the hands of heaven could get that song to me without the writer knowing what I had experienced with Sophia. That song to me was a confirmation, and I still believe to this day that my best days are still ahead of me.

A Speck of Light Getting Bright

When you come off of a show like *American Idol*, a lot of people in the music industry don't consider you a "real" musician. In their minds, you didn't pay your dues. Success appears to come easy, but I knew differently. They didn't get to see the eight years doing whatever I could to get my music career started. They didn't see the hours and hours I put in driving a truck and working two jobs to get where I was today. I didn't let it bother me. I tried to keep my eyes on what I knew was important and continue the momentum that had started.

A lot of work goes into the promotion of a record. We did a radio tour after the release of every single from my first album. In a lot of ways, radio rules the world when it comes to music success. The music programmers control what's going to be played on the air, so these tours were really important—and pretty exhausting.

As you know, morning shows don't start in the afternoon, and I am not a morning person. I was constantly getting up at five to go on morning shows and talk about my album. I went to a hundred different radio stations in about four months to campaign for them to play my songs. I was doing shows at night, too, singing for fans and doing what I loved: entertaining. I met people who wanted to shake my hand, have me kiss their babies, and even change diapers. (Okay, maybe not the last one, but I sure was asked to do some crazy things at times.) Sometimes it felt like I was some kind of political figure or something. Everywhere I went, people wanted my autograph. They wanted to take pictures with me. Places I had always watched on TV were now places I had the opportunity to perform at, and people recognized who I was. It made me feel wanted and loved. I felt as if everything I had ever experienced up until now had paid off.

I've had the opportunity to open for artists such as Sugarland, Tim McGraw, Lady Antebellum, and Taylor Swift. I've performed at the Grand Ole Opry, where I was able to take the Sophia's Heart Nashville kids choir to sing with me. I had the privilege of meeting influential people such as former president George W. Bush and Joel and Victoria Osteen. I was taken aback when Victoria told me she had enjoyed watching me on *American Idol.*

While I was on tour with Sugarland, I found out my first single was in the Top 25. It felt amazing. Maybe all those radio tours paid off. I couldn't believe the things that were unfolding before my very eyes.

When you have hope, you have an energy that recharges you and drives you. But when I was caught up in the midst of my depression, I felt like a zombie at times. I was numb and couldn't feel anything except pain. Now all of that had changed. Hope is the light at the end of the tunnel. In the beginning, all you see is a speck of light. As you get closer to it, the light becomes brighter and more pronounced. Soon you find yourself at the end of the tunnel and about to step into a beautiful world again. It was a speck of light getting bright. I had nothing but excitement and anticipation for what was ahead.

It had been a long road up to this point, but things were finally coming together. Even now, I often stop and think about what would've happened if I'd let my pain stop me. What if I hadn't tried out for *American Idol* when I didn't want to? What if I had given in to the dark thoughts in my life? I never would've gotten to where I was. I never would've lived out the opportunities that were ahead of me. Where would I be today? It's a sobering thought.

Believing in hope allowed me to experience these things because I walked in the direction of my future and toward hope.

Another Plan

My second single, "I Will Not Say Goodbye," got to number thirty-two on the charts. While that may be respectable, it was not exactly where we had hoped it would go. I knew that wasn't enough for the record label. I knew they wanted more. I did too. It was frustrating.

We had previously discussed creating more of a soulful sound on my album, but it was tamed while working with the producers. I couldn't help but wonder if that was part of the problem. I'm sure there were a lot of factors that were in play. I sat down with the record executives and told them we needed to capture more of my soulful tone. That's what people saw on the show, and that's what they expected from me. To do a more toned-down version of me didn't feel right. We decided to record a new single, "Second Hand Heart," and release it to see where things would go from there.

My third single did not do well at all. That was a sign that things were starting to get scary. In September 2011, I got a phone call right before we were planning to shoot the video for "Second Hand Heart." Sony had chosen to drop me.

Strangely, in that moment, I wasn't discouraged. God has a way of preparing you for transitions in life that come. You may not always see it at the time, but there is another plan at work. The expectation of how life should play out is rarely the reality. It all comes down to a choice to keep moving forward in hope. The key is to keep pressing forward until the hope shines through.

Around the same time, my manager started working on other things too. I started sensing a disconnect. My gut instinct was preparing me for what was to come. He called me a few months after Sony dropped my contract and told me he didn't feel like he was doing me any favors by keeping me as a client and that he was just holding me back, so he decided to part ways with me as well.

Once again, I felt a strange calm. Yes, there were times of discouragement in the days ahead. I didn't know what this would mean for my music career. All the hard work leading up to this point was suddenly on pause. And, yes, it took me longer to get where I am today because of what happened. But I didn't focus on those things. I knew there was more to come for me, so I started moving in that direction. I had seen too many good things in my past come together to believe it would suddenly stop now. Sometimes what you know in your heart is strong enough to override the doubt, so I pressed on.

Hope Comes Into Play

When we are right in the middle of difficult things, it's hard to have perspective. We are so close to the details that we can't see in front of us or even what is around us. We can't see what's coming, and sometimes we can't make sense of what just happened.

Eagles are an amazing species of birds. They are large, powerful, and fast. Humanity has been fascinated with eagles for a long time. There are stories from Greek mythology as well as many of the world's religions. This bird, being the largest and most significant, has a heavy beak for hunting and killing its prey and is able to carry the largest load of any known bird on record.

There is something that has fascinated me about eagles for a long time. I think it is their expansive wings and the ease by which they can fly through the air. I rarely see eagles close to the ground; I see them high in trees or flying in the sky.

I often wonder what it is like to see life through the eyes of an eagle. Sometimes when I'm on an airplane, I will look out the window as we get ready to land and wonder if what I'm looking at is similar to what the eagle sees. Eagles are powerful and mysterious creatures with acute eyesight.

It isn't until we are able to rise above the difficult situation that we begin to see how the seemingly random dots are connected in just the right way to position you for what's next. This is how the eagle views things, and we should remind ourselves of this perspective often. What you see and experience now should always be taken into context of the bigger picture.

The challenge is that you may not have access to the bigger picture until you are a little further down the road. This is where hope comes into play. Hope gives us the ability to connect the dots before they are connected. The reality is that you may be the only one who can see that through the eyes of your heart—for now.

For a long time, people saw me differently.

Most people saw me as only a worship leader and a truck driver.

I saw myself on the world's stage.

Most people saw me only as someone who barely made it through high school. I saw myself as someone who had the skills and resolve to be successful in business.

Most people saw me only as someone who had lost his wife early in life. In time, I saw that painful experience as the catalyst that resulted in Sophia's Heart, an organization that is changing lives daily by helping people discover hope again.

We can see only what is before us. It is rarely more than our perception, and perception is often very different from reality. Hope transforms our perspective from the ground level to the picture of our lives from an eagle's perspective when it flies over the earth. It is only then that we can see how the roller coaster we've been riding is less chaotic and more controlled than we ever thought. It is only then we can see a clear beginning and a clear end.

There is a plan for your life. It is bigger than you ever imagined. It is greater than what you planned. It is more significant than you ever thought was possible. But it all hinges on whether or not we'll be courageous enough to embrace a lifestyle of hope or continue to randomly go through life wishing for the best.

Something to Look Forward To

When Sony dropped my contract, I suddenly found myself with more free time—something that was scarce in my post-*Idol* days. Many artists might've gotten discouraged when the team disappeared and the crowds thinned, but I saw things differently. I had purpose.

Even though some people I really thought I needed dropped me, I knew I had to believe that something better would come out of it. Sometimes you have to let those things happen and just let them play out. I knew deep down inside that more good was still to come.

Purpose makes anything you do way better. Even if you're working in what feels like the worst job in the world, you can find purpose and it will help you start thinking that job may not be so bad after all. It's amazing what hope and purpose can do to your perspective. It can move you toward a better future.

I have always seen my music as a movement, and Sophia's Heart is integral to that vision. Although I would have chosen at the time to continue on the path I was on and grow from there, things took a different turn. The apparent setback gave me the time I needed to focus on a new piece of my musical vision: establishing Sophia's Heart to be a thriving nonprofit. I had something to look forward to. I had renewed purpose, and it kept me moving forward in hope.

When the calls came and the people fell away, the choice to move ahead was the only real option. I could not see where the road would take me. I had to swing at the curveball thrown my way. Right now, while I'm working on this book, I'm also working on a new album. At times the delay in my music career was as tedious as watching paint dry, but it's all coming together better than it ever has before. How many artists get the second chance I'm getting?

When you look at your life in retrospect, you start realizing there is a bigger story being written. I had to trust things to work out instead of fighting it and getting frustrated when things didn't work out the way I thought they should have. The Author of my life has written new chapters that have created my story exactly as it needs to be. There was another plan — a better plan than what I had envisioned. Had I been discouraged or bitter, things might've turned out differently or I might have been jaded about the whole music business. Hope helped me stay on the right path. With hope, when other people think you've failed, you know inside you haven't.

People often have timelines for when they think things will happen, but a lot of things in your life are not going to happen in your timing, and you have to be okay with that. It doesn't mean it isn't going to happen. Although I've seen and experienced a lot of amazing things, I feel that the best days of my career are yet to be seen.

To this day, I still have a good relationship with my old manager and my old label company. Two years ago, I didn't know what would happen and what good things were still to come, but I hoped for it. Hope is the key. You have to hope there's something better coming or you won't move toward it.

A Glimpse of a Bigger Picture

Scars show where you have been, but they don't have to determine where you are going. They may leave a mark, but they don't have to hold you back. What you do next is more important than what you did—or didn't do—yesterday.

It is an energizing feeling when we get a glimpse of a bigger picture and a greater plan, but that experience also comes with challenges. Our lives can be a lot like jigsaw puzzles. They come to us in a container of a thousand pieces. On the cover is this beautiful picture. But before we can see the picture ourselves, we have to understand how all the pieces fit together. We try, make mistakes, and have to undo incorrect connection points until we make the right choices and create the beautiful picture on the cover.

Everything that happened to me during this time told me that a bigger change had taken place in my life. The pieces I was carrying around in a box were looking less like a jigsaw puzzle and more like the picture on the cover.

Once you have the pieces in place, you don't unlink them unless you are ready to quit altogether. Life is no different. It comes to us in a lot of pieces that take a lot of time, energy, and effort to make sense of. Once we do have that sense of what has happened, is happening, and will happen, we recognize we must continue to build and move forward. If we don't, we'll get stuck and never realize the beauty and the blessing before us.

Your life is a beautiful picture you have yet to fully realize. There are likely some pieces you've been able to put together on your own. Others you have discovered through circumstances and people who have brought you the wisdom and the pain you needed at the time to make the connection.

As you continue on, you realize that what you're putting together is revealing something even more beautiful than you first had in mind. This is what I mean when I talk about your divine destiny. It is already built within you. The experiences you go through reveal your destiny in pieces. Sometimes it requires radical moves and carefully rethinking how the pieces fit together. Sometimes it comes together quickly and with little effort. Either way, you are moving forward and getting closer to the big picture you first saw on the box.

Don't allow your pain to prevent you from reaching forward.

Don't allow your perspective to inhibit your ability to see the big picture.

You are more than your pain.

You are bigger, stronger, and more creative than you've ever imagined.

You have an exciting future to embrace. It's never too late to begin again. Allow hope to strengthen you, and lean into the future that is before you. You'll be amazed how the momentum will sweep you up and how quickly the pieces of the puzzle will become a beautiful picture of your divine destiny.

Scan for a sneak peek of new music from Danny.

Chapter 14

When Passions Collide

Leave a legacy by investing in others.

Life is short. But a life that invests in others lives on forever. Our presence remains long after we leave this earth through the stories shared among those whom we loved and served.

Sophia's life was cut short, but that didn't mean she couldn't live on in some way. Yes, she would always be present in my heart. Yes, her family and those she loved would never forget her. But what about those people who never had the opportunity to meet her? How would they share in the love and concern she had for others, especially children?

Sophia and I both had big dreams for what life would be like for us in the future. I wanted a music career. She wanted to finish school and become a full-time teacher. We both thought we had lots of time to figure out the details, and we always assumed we would do it together.

Dreams are powerful vehicles for discovering our purpose. They reveal part of ourselves that we tend to overlook and confirm things that we hope for but often fail to consider as possible. When we allow our dreams to speak to us, we discover the strength to act in the midst of uncertainty, pain, and doubt.

Keeping Her Alive

Shortly after I lost Sophia, the principal where Sophia had worked as a teaching assistant asked me to meet. He explained there was a small health insurance policy through the school that had a death benefit. I wasn't aware of it, and I don't think Sophia even knew about it. This was a surprise.

At first I was offended that some faceless company had reduced my wife to a dollar figure. Then I realized the money would give me an opportunity to honor her in a special way. The craziest part is that Sophia and I had changed to her benefits just a year before she passed away to save money each month. Before that, we were on my health insurance benefits, and I'm pretty sure it didn't include a death benefit. I took it as a sign that this money meant something bigger.

The total insurance benefit was $39,000. I know that doesn't sound like a lot of money, but at the time, I didn't have an income. I had quit both my jobs. I could have easily justified keeping every dollar of that policy. Instead, I wanted to find a way to make sure Sophia's heart and passion for helping others lived on forever. People may never get a chance to meet Sophia in person, but I wanted them to be touched by her love just like I was and all the people who knew her. I knew the money wasn't mine to keep.

I also wanted to give her family a gift. Her family had welcomed me in. The first time I met her dad, I had just turned seventeen. I had lived nearly half my life knowing and being around Sophia's family. I knew they were suffering inside from losing a daughter and sister just like I was suffering from losing a spouse. I wanted to do something that ensured Sophia would never be forgotten. Her life on earth may have been cut short because of an unfortunate tragedy, but I was determined that wasn't going to be the end of her impact on this earth.

Keeping that insurance benefit never even crossed my mind. It was never a legitimate option for me. I knew I had to use that money to keep Sophia's legacy alive.

Carrying Sophia's Name

I was given a CD by a nonprofit consultant who suggested I listen to Matthew Barnett's story. It was a powerful one.

Matthew has an incredible story of breaking out of the normal flow of his life to follow a dream. He is the son of a well-known and respected pastor in Arizona, Tommy Barnett. Matthew felt called to ministry, but it is a very different ministry from his dad's. He took over a small church in the hood of Los Angeles. The first day of his ministry at that church, there was a murder on the front steps.

One day Matthew felt compelled to walk around the community to see what was going on and who lived there. He noticed prostitutes, drug dealers, and addicts. These were the people few people understood or had a desire to reach. But Matthew felt this was his church and these were the people he needed to focus on and help, so he turned his entire attention to building an outreach center of hope for the hopeless.

Matthew Barnett and the Dream Center have done amazing work in Los Angeles. Today the Dream Center is a thriving organization that has captured the hearts of so many people who desire to lead a life of significance. I only hoped I would be able to do something significant with my life like Matthew has done with his.

It was not an easy road. For many years, Matthew faced hardship. But he has created something significant and is impacting lives in real and practical ways.

I had the opportunity to meet Matthew while I was taping

American Idol in Los Angeles. I took a cab to see the Dream Center for myself and met Matthew in person. It was unbelievable, and Matthew was so humble and gracious. He became like a big brother to me and some of the other contestants. When we were in town, he would check on us just to make sure we were doing okay.

After hearing Matthew's story, I knew I wanted to do something similar. And to ensure Sophia lived on, I wanted something that carried her name. I wanted to be sure the people we helped experienced the love Sophia had for everyone and the kindness with which she treated others.

A Legacy Preserved

There is something special about investing in a child. Sophia always saw the potential in the little ones who were drawn to her. She believed that if you put the seed of hope within children when they were young, it would sprout to something beautiful when they got older. Sophia thought a child was a window to heaven.

The innocence, courage, excitement, and love of a child are contagious. Sophia and I both loved kids and wanted to raise a family together. Unfortunately, we weren't given that opportunity. Whatever legacy Sophia would have, it had to involve children. I wouldn't have it any other way.

I never thought I would start a nonprofit, but that seemed like the logical next step. I wanted to create something at the intersection of our passions. We shared those passions together and served alongside each other as we found ways to help and serve others in a variety of ways that included feeding, clothing, and housing the hurting, helpless, and forgotten. I know our focus will diversify in the years to come, but my prayer is that we'll never forget it's all about loving others as much as we love ourselves.

Of course, just because I decided to start an organization doesn't mean all the details just came together and things started moving forward. There was still a tremendous amount of work to be done before we were an official organization and had a plan of how to accomplish our goals.

There were two challenges I faced immediately: the paperwork required to become an official nonprofit organization and getting started. On December 3, 2008, we signed the papers for Sophia's Heart to become an official nonprofit that could receive tax-deductible donations.

Milwaukee was our home. It's where Sophia and I were raised, where we were married, and where she died. At first, that is where I wanted to locate Sophia's Heart, but none of the details fell into place. The doors just weren't opening.

Sophia's sister and brother-in-law had already moved to Nashville to be part of the music scene. I knew I needed help. It wasn't going to be easy. I also wanted to involve Sophia's family in this effort because I did this in part as a way to help them through the suffering and see the good that could come from this tragedy. They were happy to help.

I wanted to lay a solid foundation. All the books I had read on business told me that the most successful organizations are built on a solid foundation. One of the first things I did after paying the lawyers to secure official nonprofit status was hire a consulting firm to help get things moving and build the organization on solid ground.

Creating Something Positive

During the initial stages of starting Sophia's Heart, I was still hurting from the loss of Sophia. It was tough for me emotionally. Every time I told someone about why this organization carried Sophia's name or how we arrived at focusing on homeless families and children, all the pain rose to the surface.

Everyone grieves differently. Some people grieve and withdraw. I was headed there, but I knew that's not how Sophia wanted me to live. I also knew the unexpected insurance policy gave me the financial capacity to multiply its impact by establishing a legacy that was consistent with the passions Sophia and I shared.

I felt like sitting in a corner and crying, but I also thought about Matthew Barnett, who believed in his dream so much he was willing to do whatever it took to bring his dream to life. I thought about Jeremy Camp, who in the face of tragedy still believed in himself and worked to transform his pain into helping and serving others.

I thought about the ordinary people who said yes when the right opportunities came along, and I knew I had to move forward and create something positive in the midst of all this pain and suffering. When you build other people's dreams, you will build your own. It is strange to think about, but the truth of the matter is we can't heal ourselves. It's impossible, and it's not how we were created.

It is in our giving that we experience blessing the most.

It is in our moving forward that we find relief from our grieving.

It is in our loving that we are made complete.

It is in our serving that we are healed.

I wanted to give up and give in to the pain so many times, but I didn't. I knew the only way to have any kind of peace in the midst of Sophia's death was to make sure that what excited her the most, what brought her the most pleasure, and what she dreamed about would come into reality. I would have preferred to do this with her, but in a way I feel like I am.

Sophia's Heart ensured that her legacy was preserved forever—in the warmth of a blanket, the safety of a home, and the smile and love of a child.

I thank God for Sophia's Heart. It gave me something to live for again. Instead of focusing on the darkness of my pain, I was reminded that investing in others brings healing and leaves a legacy for many.

Power to Influence

Someone else who has personally inspired me is George Müller, a man who gave his life to helping orphans in England. Even though he lived during the nineteenth century, his legacy was an inspiration to me. His emphasis on orphans and the poor, especially concerning education, was criticized. Yet throughout his life, he housed, fed, and educated thousands of orphans who were once living on the street and ignored by society.

Like George Müller, I want to spend my life, money, and opportunities helping others rise above their current situations. I truly believe there are no limits that can hold us back when we believe in ourselves and recognize the divine hope and purpose inside of us. If we all did this right where we are with what we have, we could change the world.

I am not impressed by people with money, power, or positions of authority. Those things are only temporary. I am impressed by ordinary people who attempt to do radical things that change the world in a positive way. When I think about people like that, I think about Abraham Lincoln, Martin Luther King Jr., and Mother Teresa. These are people who saw an opportunity to help someone else and said yes to the opportunity. We could change our lives if we decided to say yes to opportunities to help others. Most of the time we are focused on what will help us. There is a multiplying factor that comes into play when we give what we have to helping others in need.

You don't have to be the president of the United States, a Catholic nun, or a social-movement leader to make a difference. People are easily distracted by the extraordinary. They think that if they can't do big things, they won't be able to make a difference. That is not true at all. You don't need a college degree or infinite resources to make a difference; you just need a willing heart. The most powerful change we can make is when we choose to use our power to influence others, no matter where we do it, in big or small ways. It all rests within our decision to say yes.

Choose Your Reward

If your focus is on leaving a lasting legacy, then your purpose is not to win short-term approval but to treat each person as another human being who is in need.

My reward will be in a life that has been changed for the good. When I see lives restored, marriages put back together, children discovering joy again, addictions broken, and depression lifted, that's when I know I am building the right kind of legacy and will earn a reward no human or industry can manufacture.

Ancient wisdom teaches us that a great name is to be valued among all things in life. I think the clearest path to greatness (which I understand to be significance) is to love the people in your life. Show kindness to those who are like you and who aren't like you. Give generously of your time and money, even if you don't think you have a lot to give. Don't wait for opportunities to come along before you help others; create them. We can all give something no matter where we are in life, even if it's just a kind word or a smile.

It's hard to tell what the future holds. It's difficult to predict if I will be in the music business for the rest of my life. Only a select few can survive a lifetime in a business that is quick to praise you and even quicker to forget about you.

I have already had to watch my first love die. If I ever question what's really important, I don't have to look too far to be reminded that love is what really matters. When we really love other people, we will give ourselves away. And something strange happens when we give ourselves away again and again and again; we never run out of love to give.

When you don't have love and you do good things, your reward is the attention of others, and that never truly helps anyone. When you have love and you invest in the things that last forever, your reward will outlast your days on earth. Leave a lasting legacy by investing in others. Bet on the things in life that are eternal. Love others on purpose. The rest will fade away.

Chapter 15

A Relentless Challenge

If you give up too early,
you will forfeit the gift of helping others.

Obstacles should be welcomed. They clarify our ideas, test our resolve, and focus our efforts. If we do not survive, then we move on. If we choose to continue, then we know it is because we have no other option but to push through whatever is between us and the realization of our deepest desires.

How many times have we missed the blessing of the moment, person, or experience because we were looking for things to happen our way? There is one thing I can say with certainty: Life is full of obstacles and struggle. What we do when presented with those obstacles is what will determine our experiences in life. Will they be full, or will we leave a part of our divine destiny on the table because the uncertainty, fear, or even our own stubbornness and doubt keeps us from facing anything that seems too big, too scary, or too impossible?

It isn't until we choose to act that life begins to support us and carry us forward. The words you need come in the moment. The insight you're waiting on comes in the moment of decision. The next step becomes clear as we begin to move forward.

Expect challenges. Anticipate pain. Embrace uncertainty. These are the ingredients to leaving a legacy that will live beyond this present life.

Come Together

I wish I could say that when Sophia's Heart became an official nonprofit at the end of 2008, I waved my hand and—*poof*—everything came together. Without hesitation, I can tell you it didn't happen that way. In fact, it was such a slow start that even I began to wonder if all the details would ever come together.

Everything about the start-up process moved very slowly. There were a lot of details to be covered. And the timing was difficult because I was on *American Idol* in 2009 and on tour for most of 2010 and 2011. I was certainly supported by a great team, but it's hard to help others see what's inside your head when you aren't physically present most of the time. My brother-in-law did great work, and he did a lot of it while on tour with me. I'm grateful.

We also had a huge interruption as a result of a natural disaster no one saw coming. We were just getting our music and arts program going when an epic flood hit Nashville in May 2010. It was downright hell on earth for a few weeks in Nashville, depending on what part of the city you lived in.

One of the consultants I had originally hired to help with Sophia's Heart and later brought on staff full-time encouraged me to organize some type of response to the flood. At first I didn't see how we would be able to do much with what we had at the time. But we didn't allow our current circumstances and limited resources to stop us from doing something to help.

We contacted the company Best Buy and were able to use an

abandoned store facility for one dollar. People donated thousands of items. It seemed the entire city was in disaster-response mode. It was an unbelievable event to be part of.

In addition to acquiring food, clothes, cleanup kits, furniture, and essential supplies, we set up a makeshift computer lab that had Internet connection so people could connect with family members. More important, they could also begin the application process through FEMA for financial assistance. Near the facility was a well-known homeless community called tent city. We made sure their needs were taken care of too. All in all, we were able to help 450 families through this effort and operated out of that building for almost four months.

I learned a valuable lesson through all of this: Never wait for the perfect time to help others. That time usually doesn't come. Start where you are and take a step of faith that the details will be worked out as you go. Sometimes all you need is an idea.

My goal was not to do this so I could get recognition; I wanted this to be about Sophia's Heart. The circumstances were devastating. However, our quick response did bring an awareness among the city's nonprofit and business leadership that would likely have taken years. Good things can come even in the midst of the worst circumstances. When your efforts are focused on others, the light sometimes gets shined on you. And that's what happened for Sophia's Heart.

It wasn't an easy choice to start my own organization. There were so many times I questioned if I had made the right decision. As we faced the usual difficulties, I often wondered if I'd made it too hard on myself by starting from scratch. It would've been easier to partner with another organization already in existence. But now, years down the road, I feel confident that Sophia's Heart is well worth all the hardships and was the right choice for me.

Unexpected Generosity

Best Buy was gracious to allow us to use their facility for the relief efforts, but it was never the intention to be located there forever. We knew we needed to find a location of our own. But we had no idea where to begin. It wasn't like we had endless resources. There were lots of people who wanted to talk to us because they thought we had deep pockets. Their intentions were revealed quickly.

People recognized me from *American Idol*. Obviously, some thought I made a lot of money on the show and had lots to spend. When looking for facilities for Sophia's Heart, architects and builders were excited to talk to me because of what they thought I had. I learned to become very clear in my expectations. Eventually, those people went away.

One offer came from an organization that was deeply invested in serving the needs of others in their community. The leader of this organization spoke with great enthusiasm about how we could partner together. He had the facilities, and we had the idea. I wish I could say it was that easy. It wasn't.

Things became complicated the deeper we got into the details. It was clear to me this wasn't going to work—ever. The enthusiasm we all had about the situation had faded, and it seemed that we needed to go back to square one.

I was devastated. I can't say I felt like giving up, but it did feel impossible. It seemed like the perfect solution at the time. The more I thought about it later, though—as often happens the further you move away from "perfect" situations—I realized the partnership would have been less than desirable in many ways.

Sometimes we get mad when things don't work out, but we fail to recognize that maybe we haven't discovered the real blessing yet. Just because something looks like a blessing doesn't mean it is one. The same afternoon that the other details fell apart, I received a random voicemail from a guy who said he owned a medical facility he wanted to donate to a nonprofit and was calling to see if we were interested. My answer was a resounding yes.

Dreams Do Come True

We were originally supposed to meet the owner of the building (the man who left me the voicemail) and his real estate agent to tour the facility. When we arrived, it was just the real estate agent. I had just been burned, so I was going to be really disappointed if it happened again.

The building had everything we wanted. It had a big utility kitchen. It had office space separate from the rest of the building. It had fifty big rooms with full-functioning bathrooms. It had a large lobby, clinical space, and a cafeteria. I became more and more excited, and my heart jumped inside me. I was almost in tears because I couldn't believe this was actually happening. I tried to play it cool on the outside, but I knew inside this was the place that would house Sophia's Heart and give us a chance to really make a difference.

It was finally time to dive into the details. I learned early in life that if it's too good to be true, it probably is. I was really hoping this was not the case. The real estate agent changed the story just slightly from what the guy had said in his voicemail. Instead of it being a direct donation, he said the donation amounted to fifty percent of the total cost of the building. That meant we would have to come up with about $750,000 for the other half. Impossible.

We left that meeting feeling defeated. We barely even had 5 percent of what he was asking in our bank account. I told the few of us who had been on the tour that if we were meant to have this building, the details would work themselves out. I'm not sure if I felt the need to say that because I needed to say something a good leader would say or if I was trying to convince myself of the same thing too.

A few weeks passed by. Nothing. Then I finally met with the owner of the building. We met at a golf club, and after spending the afternoon with this guy, I knew that what I had heard about this man was true: He was very, very successful.

We eventually got around to talking about the hospital facility.

I explained what the real estate agent had said. I told him we didn't have $750,000 to pay for the building. He paused and then looked directly at me. He said the building was ours if we wanted it. But he was also clear in saying that this 77,000-square-foot facility was *all ours*, which meant he didn't want us coming back to ask for money to make repairs or because we couldn't afford the utility costs.

Of course I said yes. I told him I would pour everything I had into this building and would do whatever it took. Although I was serious, he wasn't impressed. He just wanted assurance we would make his donation worthwhile. He had other organizations that wanted the building, but somehow we got it.

The important details were in place. Now we just needed to get this deal in writing, transfer the deed of ownership, and begin building Sophia's Heart in the way we had dreamed about all along.

Of course, there were more obstacles. The closing date kept being pushed back. During that time, we thought we might lose the building. The real estate agent said many times that he had more than one cash buyer who was ready to move. We also discovered that someone was subleasing a wing of the facility. They would become our tenant. It wasn't perfect, but we hoped it wouldn't be forever.

The day finally came. After all the anticipating, pushing, and praying, the closing date arrived. We signed the papers on the building on November 15, 2010. I was in shock. We actually had a facility. A 77,000-square-foot facility. It was time to start making our dreams—and the dreams of so many others we wanted to help—come true. In that moment, Matthew Barnett and the Dream Center immediately came to mind. Maybe Sophia's Heart could have a similar impact on the Nashville community that Matthew has had in Los Angeles. That was certainly my prayer, and now we had a physical address to locate the dream I had been carrying with me in my heart for so long.

A Clarifying Experience

Again, I wish I could say everything was perfect after that, but it was not the case. Instead, the heat was turned up on the situation in a way we never could have anticipated. When the community found out we were moving in, many of its residents and business owners were not happy.

To say we were met with some opposition would be an understatement. East Nashville is a community in transition. Poverty and wealth exist side by side. There are still many troubled parts of East Nashville.

Many nonprofits and church groups had come and gone with good intentions. They would show up, distribute food and clothes, and then leave. These kinds of past events brought a transient crowd of people into the community who didn't always treat other people's property with respect. This community was trying to revitalize the area, but these efforts had complicated the process.

Our original plan was to launch a soup kitchen and start giving away clothing. We were going to relocate the music and arts program there, too. When we went to file the necessary papers related to use of the building, the word spread like wildfire. Soon there were community meetings calling our intentions into question. People weren't happy about our vision. There were huge signs going up that included the personal phone number of one of my staff members and a website to boycott us.

It was really a clarifying experience. It caused me to check my intentions. Just because we think that what we're doing is right doesn't mean it is. So many organizations that came in before us came one day and left the next. I'm not trying to put down what they were doing, but it was more about them than the people they were trying to help. We listened to the criticism from the community, and we became a stronger organization because of it.

We quickly redesigned our plan of action. We engaged the community leaders who seemed to be leading the movement against us. And our efforts proved to be wise. It didn't take too long to convince even the biggest skeptics that we were in this for the long haul. This was not a glorified collect-and-dump effort. We were not moving in to move out. We were committed to a better community by helping homeless families find the help they need to turn their lives around. We wanted to be a breath of fresh air for the community, not make things worse.

Since then, we've experienced no opposition from the community. Sometimes opposition isn't a horrible thing. Sometimes it can be used to clarify our intentions and place us in a better position to care for and serve people.

Overcoming Challenges

The challenge of any nonprofit—big and small—is always funding. There never seems to be enough. It's hard to raise money for an organization when it doesn't have a lot of hard outcomes. We could show progress, but we needed more money to fund the programs that were going to create the outcomes we were looking for. Money usually follows outcomes, but we needed money to create the outcomes.

I decided from the beginning I would never take a salary from Sophia's Heart, and I never will. I never want what Sophia's Heart is doing to be called into question over financial integrity. I've seen it happen too many times, and I didn't want any part of it. In fact, in most years, I am one of the biggest donors of Sophia's Heart. I believe that will not be the case forever because I know we will capture the hearts of some financial leaders who want to make a tremendous difference in the lives of families and want to support our work. But that's how much we believe in this organization. We do what is needed to keep the dream alive.

We also had to clean up the building. The medical company that previously occupied the facility did not clean it up before they left, and we had to do it ourselves. It wasn't easy, but we were determined not to let anything stand in our way.

There are, of course, some other expenses that come with owning a large facility like the one we inherited. The fire inspector came through and uncovered about $15,000 of repairs that needed to be completed. The operating expenses alone were overwhelming. We finally discovered a system that allowed us to keep the building warm in the places where it was necessary and not heat or cool the spaces we weren't utilizing yet. Even with our planning, it is still an overwhelming amount of money needed every month just to operate the facilities.

I knew we'd have to overcome many challenges to make this dream a reality, but it would be so worth it in the end.

Lives Changed

We moved in our first homeless family—a mom, dad, and five children—in 2011. We focused exclusively on families. Most homeless families end up being split up because a lot of facilities are not set up for families. They may provide food and shelter, but it further increases the stress of the situation. And the ones who really lose in this scenario are the children.

At Sophia's Heart, our goal is to take the hospital rooms and make them into one-room efficiency apartments. All the elements are there: large rooms, HVAC, and full bathrooms. We want these families to have a place where they feel safe and escape from the brutal world they are trying to tame as they work to become self-sustaining again.

We were able to help more than twenty-five families in 2012. Once our Nashville facility is completely renovated, we'll be able to take between eighty and a hundred families off the streets each year and give them a safe, warm, and comfortable place to heal and reposition their lives for future success. With the facility we have, our growth potential is incredible.

Good things are happening. Volunteers and donors are helping transform the facility one room at a time, while others are involved in direct family care.

Sophia's Heart couldn't do all that we do without our incredible staff. Their stories are so inspirational. Only a few staff members are paid. And those positions aren't paid what they are worth. These people aren't there for the money; they're there because they buy into the vision.

We have volunteers who come in from time to time to generously offer their time and skills. We also have live-in volunteers who give their lives to help these families around the clock. While we do help with their expenses, they get no salary. There is no way we could do what we do without them. These are the real champions who should be praised, admired, and applauded. Their constant devotion to the families we help is the reason lives are being changed every day at Sophia's Heart.

In addition to providing a safe place to live, food to eat, and clean clothes, we help these families develop career skills, complete their GEDs, and find steady work. We also support them if they are spiritually curious, and we provide counseling when necessary. Our goal is to make them whole again so they can overcome whatever obstacles they are facing now and in the future.

One of the programs I'm deeply invested in is our dream-building class. I designed it to help these families envision a more desirable future. I personally interact with each resident in hopes of helping inspire them to reach for their goals and believe in themselves. When we have faith that good things are coming, our state of mind shifts. We begin to see the world differently, and we gain the power to change the world around us. That's what gets me most excited: seeing real people make radical adjustments and create a better future for themselves and their families.

Every Tuesday night is family night. If I am in town, this is where I am. We bring in a band, and a few singers and I perform uplifting music for the families. I find so much strength and inspiration from these gatherings where we celebrate our victories and share in our struggles. It is a beautiful picture of what I always thought the church should be.

Recently, we accepted a single mom and her son into our facility. Candace had been raised by her grandmother, who passed away while she was in high school. She was on her own after that. For a time, she was able to get a job and an apartment, but then she experienced some significant health issues and lost her job because of it. She was selling drugs and through a series of events became homeless. Candace used to keep her son at other people's houses and didn't tell anyone about being homeless because she was embarrassed. Her son finally asked her one night when they were going to have a real home. Shortly after that, she found Sophia's Heart. At first she rebelled in many ways and was afraid to trust anyone, but one of our live-in volunteers got through to her. She admitted this was the first time anyone had taken the time to listen to her since her grandma passed away. She cried as she told us that her son asked to "go home" to Sophia's Heart after experiencing the love strangers showed them at our facility. She has since successfully completed our program and graduated. She now has a steady job that pays well. She has been able to save her money and has moved to her own home. I am so happy for this family. And what makes this story even better is how she received a promotion at work and used her position to help several residents at Sophia's Heart get hired too. This is what is possible when we extend a hand to help others in need. I miss this woman and her son, but I am so proud of their journey.

We also took in a single father who came to our facility with his two kids. Thomas had previously lost his wife and experienced many hardships that left him homeless. He had moved to Nashville with the promise of a job but instead was swindled out of some money. They ended up staying in another facility that was seasonal and closed after the winter months. They were also kicked out of another place they had found to live and weren't even able to bring their belongings with them. When we accepted Thomas into our program at Sophia's Heart, he fell on his knees and cried, thanking us for helping him. He has since moved on to a stable place as well.

A story that really warms my heart is one of a single mom in nursing school. Timidly, Jennifer and her three kids came to Sophia's Heart, not knowing what to expect. She was ashamed and regretful of the decisions of her past that led her to us. Jennifer told me she had been to a few other shelters in town and had to get in line each day for that night's lodging. If she was lucky, she would get a cot for herself and her kids for the night. When she came into Sophia's Heart, our staff greeted her and handed her a key to her own room with a bathroom. When she walked into the room, the beds had new linens and there was a basket of toiletries for them, along with a welcome letter. She broke down and cried. She had never experienced this kind of reception from people who didn't even know her.

These kinds of stories—stories that have a lasting impact on me and those around me—happen every day. There are too many to tell. But these are the stories that keep me grounded. They remind me of what's important.

Pursue Your Deepest Desires

The families we serve at Sophia's Heart know how quickly the affection of others can disappear. Just see how many days you can go without a shower or clean clothes before people start looking at you strangely and treating you differently. I can tell you it isn't very long. This is why we make these families feel special and welcome. I know they don't want to be in this position. I know they are struggling with self-doubt and thoughts of failure. I've been there. That is why we strive to give them a good experience when they walk through our doors. We don't put them in a dilapidated old room; we put them in a room that is beautifully remodeled with furniture and beds that are comfortable. Our goal is to let these broken families know they're important, they are worth something, and they have a unique destiny, even if they don't feel it. Their countenance changes immediately and their mindsets begin to shift when they feel a sense of value.

There is a difference between being famous and being great. Fame fades eventually, but greatness lasts forever. The difference also lies in the source of your approval. Being famous means you are approved by the recognition and praise of others. Being great means you are approved by fulfilling and living out your deepest dream. One is temporary. One lasts forever.

The challenge is not to allow ourselves to be sidetracked by the things that don't last forever. My focus is on building up and investing in other people through personal relationships. This is what matters, and this is what lasts forever. So much of what we value in life is temporary. We should invest in people, not things. This is the only path to the abundant life.

I wish Sophia could be here to see all that has taken place. I know she would be proud. And the best is yet to come. While we continue our work in Nashville and Milwaukee, we are already exploring new cities into which we can expand our efforts.

What I have learned through this relentless challenge is that true faith means thanking God before the miracle happens and then having the resolve to see it through and watch your dreams come to life. Saying I have faith is not saying I deny the facts; it just acknowledges that God is bigger than the facts. This is what it means to live with purpose and in pursuit of our deepest desires. If we had given up on this dream of building Sophia's Heart due to the challenges we faced, we would've forfeited the gift of helping so many people and changing the lives of so many families.

Never give up. Never stop trying to accomplish your dreams. You never know how many lives will be affected by helping others in the midst of pursuing your own dreams.

Scan to hear more stories from Sophia's Heart.

Chapter 16

A New Beginning

You have yet to accomplish all you were designed to do.

The dreams you hold deep within you are the promises hope has given you to remind you that there is more in your future than you can anticipate right now. You must keep moving in the direction hope is taking you.

It may feel like you're moving backward.

It may feel like you are stumbling all over yourself.

It may feel like you've lost your way.

But then it happens in a moment: Your dreams finally come true.

My heart was empty. My life was full. I didn't know if I could love another woman the same way I loved Sophia.

In just a few short years, my wife had died unexpectedly and I had auditioned for *American Idol*, founded Sophia's Heart, finished in the top three on season 8 of *American Idol*, toured with the finalists, signed a record deal, and moved to Nashville to continue my music career. Needless to say, those years went by fast — too fast, probably.

By 2011, I started feeling the desire to share my life with someone in a way you can do only with someone you love. I didn't want to spend the rest of my life alone. But I wondered if anyone finds love twice in a lifetime. It seemed unlikely.

Starting at Square One

Dating is difficult for anyone. Add a little complexity to that by way of *American Idol*, and it becomes almost impossible.

The hard part about living your life onstage is that you sometimes question the intentions of the people around you. You never really know for sure what people are thinking or if they really like you for the right reasons. It is the blessing and curse that comes with living your life onstage.

I went through some of the same things many people do. My friends made suggestions, but I never clicked with any of those girls. I tried dating a few girls I thought were attractive, but we never really connected. I was back at square one.

The world was watching this time as I began to date. Everyone had an opinion on who I should date and marry. While I did get insight and wisdom from people I trusted and respected, I knew I had to follow my heart, even at the risk of everyone not understanding why.

Once people realized I was serious about finding the next love of my life, they became more serious about expressing their concerns. I understood where they were coming from. These were close friends and family who were looking out for me. No one would ever replace Sophia, but I was ready to experience love again. Although I knew this decision to move forward in finding love again was difficult for many close to me and Sophia, I wanted them to embrace my next steps.

As might be expected, Sophia's family was a little surprised about my interest in dating again. They were probably hit the hardest by this decision. Sophia was their daughter and sister. I did my best to assure them I would always love her.

Perhaps it was hard because it served as a reminder that Sophia was no longer alive and life continued to move forward. Either way, I've worked hard to keep a good relationship with Sophia's family, and I consider them part of my extended family. After all, I've known them for most of my life. Even though it was hard for them to hear about it, I'm so glad they understood my need to find love again with someone I could share my life with.

A Dating Service Called Twitter

I don't spend a tremendous amount of time on social media sites. I prefer connecting with people in person or by phone. I guess you could say I am a little old-school when it comes to those kinds of things. However, I do recognize that lots of people like to keep up with what's happening in my life through social media sites like Twitter and Facebook.

While reading through some different Twitter streams, I noticed a certain woman's profile linked in to someone else's tweet. Now, just so you know, I don't date girls only because they are attractive, but I'm not going to lie: This woman made a great first impression on me. I secretly wondered if this woman (named Leyicet) was the same in person as she was online. I was curious enough that I wanted to find out. So I did what every other guy would have done: I wrote to Leyicet on Twitter. She responded. And that is how Twitter went from a social media site to a dating service in my mind.

Within a few days, our tweets became e-mails and our e-mails became Skype video calls. I wanted to meet Leyicet soon after we connected online. Skype was great, but it was no substitute for the real thing. I had to meet this woman.

Just two weeks after I connected with Leyicet on Twitter, a friend of mine let me use a free ticket on American Airlines to fly to Miami to meet her. I was in Miami, and we were having dinner together and going to church. I was immediately taken aback by how real and honest Leyicet was. And, yes, she was just as pretty—if not more so—in person as she was online.

Our conversation that night was great. I lost track of time. It had been so long since that happened I had almost forgotten what that felt like. I actually felt as though a voice deep down inside of me told me she was my next wife. I thought that was ludicrous; I didn't even know this girl, but I couldn't shake it.

Getting to Know My Heart

Leyicet was a model and also worked in the music business. She was very skeptical of anyone who appeared to be a celebrity. She spent a lot of time with celebrities and was disenchanted by what she had seen and heard. Leyicet clearly understood that many celebrities live two separate lives: one onstage and another offstage.

She was very cautious when around me at first. It was important for her to get to know my heart. She wanted to make sure I was exactly who I said I was.

Leyicet was not bothered by the fact that I was married before. She was very compassionate when I shared about my loss of Sophia and how it had wrecked my life. I felt like I could tell her anything. She didn't judge me. She didn't make assumptions or jump to conclusions. She listened, affirmed, and encouraged. Most important, we shared a common faith. Leyicet didn't grow up in a home that valued faith in anything, but her faith had become a defining factor in her life just a few years before we met. One day Leyicet decided to go to church and never stopped going after that. I love her pure and innocent commitment to live a life that is consistent with what she believes is true. We both share that. My faith at times has been tainted by years of good and bad experiences in church settings, but Leyicet hadn't had her faith long enough to be tainted by anything. I find her faith story so beautiful and compelling. It wasn't long before Leyicet started coming to Nashville. The relationship was already pointing in the direction of marriage.

Lingering Voices

I love my fans. They have been so faithful to me. But when it came out that I was dating again and—more specifically—dating Leyicet, not everyone was ready for that news. Some people thought we were moving too fast, and some believed it was still too soon after losing my first wife.

I think my fans grew to love the story of Sophia so much that it felt like betrayal for me to find love again. Some took to social media to express their concern and disappointment. Some wrote letters to my management company. A few who were in my life at the time expressed their concern in person.

I completely understood the concerns. I knew some of it was because they saw only the Danny they knew on *American Idol*. But as you know from this book, that is just part of my story. Every person on TV or on a stage is more than what they appear to be. I also knew that some people were reacting because they didn't want to see me get hurt again.

I'm so grateful for these people, but I had to shut down the voices of those trying to stand in the way of what Leyicet and I knew was right, even some of my close friends.

There will always be people who think they know better than you do about your own life. Many times people—even the closest of friends—will try to disrupt the good things going on in your life. You have to check their motivations. Is it because they see a different future for you, or is their concern valid? Once you weigh your decision, you have to trust that you know what is true, good, and right for you. No one else can decide what is best for you.

I knew once my fans and close friends had the opportunity to get to know Leyicet, they would fall in love with her as much as I had. She is such a genuine person who cares about the things I care about and is interested in the things I am interested in. We share a similar life perspective. And she fell in love with Sophia's Heart almost immediately. It wasn't long before the concern of my fans turned to congratulations.

My Big Plan

It took only seven months from the first time we met to realize we were meant for each other. We were engaged on October 14, 2011. My engagement to Leyicet didn't happen with the same public fanfare as my engagement with Sophia, but we wanted it that way.

I wanted my engagement to Leyicet to be special, so I planned a night for her, complete with a car service. I was dressed to the nines in a suit. Leyicet had always asked me to wear a suit to church, but I'd never wanted to. She had never seen me wear a suit, so I bought a new suit just for this night.

I had talked to her dad earlier in the day to ask for her hand in marriage, but there was a little language barrier because her dad doesn't speak English. He finally decided he wanted me to ask her mother because I understood her mother's Spanish much better. (I also think in his heart he didn't want to give up his daughter yet.)

Her mother was at work, so I had to rush over to where she was working, explain the situation, and get her permission. Her mother broke down crying at work and said yes. Now I actually had to execute my plans.

With fifteen or twenty minutes to spare before I was supposed to meet Leyicet, I had received her family's permission and blessing. I had a car service pick her up and meet me at an elegant restaurant. We enjoyed a beautiful ocean-side dinner and then went to the ballet. I had already planned to take her to the beach to propose, but she played right into my plans and suggested we take a walk by the ocean.

I had a friend in town and had arranged for him to meet me

there and play guitar while I sang a song that her mom used to sing to her as a little girl. Lucky for me, when I sang that song on *American Idol*, it was one of my better moments. The song was "You Are So Beautiful" by Joe Cocker.

Little did I know the wind would be blowing that evening and my friend who was playing guitar would lose his sheet music in the first verse of the song. Apparently, he didn't know the song by heart, so I just kept singing as he struggled with the notes. As a singer, that was the worst, but I made it through. I asked Leyicet to marry me, and she said yes. I was thrilled.

A Wedding or Two

Wedding planning is always exciting and a little hectic getting all the details in place. One key element is getting the marriage certificate. Leyicet and I made plans to go to the office and fill out all the paperwork together.

What should have been a fun and joyful next step in the process turned out to be a challenging day for me. I was pretty quiet, and I knew Leyicet could tell something was off. We filled out all the paperwork and turned it in. And as we walked out of the building, this well of emotion overflowed in me and I began to cry. I cried so hard I collapsed against the side of the building. I can only imagine what Leyicet must've been thinking.

Once I was able to gain my composure, I tried to explain. I never thought I would do this part of my life twice. I guess it just hit me. I tried to reassure Leyicet it had nothing to do with her and I was thrilled to be taking this step with her, but I know it had to feel awful. She was nothing but gracious and understanding.

Healing from loss is a process, and there have been other times when moments like this have come up. I'm so thankful for Leyicet, who accepts who I am and where I've been and walks with me as those moments arise.

I wanted to give Leyicet the wedding of her dreams. We were planning a public wedding for January 2012, but we wanted a more intimate setting. I knew what it was going to be like this time around, and I didn't want anything to get in the way of our special day.

We went back and forth on whether we wanted to move the wedding date up or simply elope. Randomly, Leyicet remembered my telling her that George Müller—someone who deeply inspired me, as I mentioned before—married his second wife on November 30. Our calendar was free on that date. We decided we would keep the public wedding in January but go ahead with a private ceremony on November 30, 2011. It was a very special day that we shared with just three close friends who also served as witnesses. We then left for our honeymoon in the Dominican Republic.

A few months later, we celebrated our wedding again with a public ceremony on January 29, 2012. In spite of my certainty of marrying Leyicet, yet again there were some nagging criticisms from various parties who were concerned for me. After our ceremony, however, more than $35,000 in donations came in for Sophia's Heart. I took that as a confirmation that those people understood my moving forward in love was the right choice. I knew Sophia would've wanted me to find love again. I also knew she was honored that day in memory and spirit, just as she is every day through the work of the organization that carries her name.

People often ask Leyicet how she deals with the memory of Sophia always being part of our lives. I love her response. She has never been jealous, truly. She understands I have a past and doesn't want to diminish that in any way.

What she often says is that Sophia loved a Danny that Leyicet never knew. They both loved two very different men, so there is no need to be jealous. Danny and Sophia were right for each other in that time of their lives in those formative years. The Danny Leyicet knows and loves has had the benefit of those years of experience and is a different person today because of it.

There have been many times in which Leyicet was mistaken for Sophia. It must've been awkward for Leyicet in those moments, but she handled them with grace. Our marriage has been all I had hoped it would be. We care for each other, support each other, and complement each other in so many ways. My love for Leyicet is not diminished because I was married once before. This was an opportunity for a new beginning and a new life. I am happier now than ever.

From the Outside In

After Leyicet and I got married, I decided to sell the first house I had bought when I moved to Nashville. A small mortgage was the only debt I had at that time, and I felt the urge again to become debt-free. I wasn't sure how quickly it was going to sell, given the state of the economy at the time.

Our real estate agent had an open house the same day we put our house on the market. Within three weeks, we had a cash offer that we accepted. It was unbelievable. And then in the middle of our celebration, we remembered that we hadn't quite settled on the details of where we were going to live.

We were scrambling to look for a house, but we couldn't find the right one. And I don't like to make big decisions too quickly. That is one way I stay out of financial trouble.

So Leyicet and I decided to move into our facility at Sophia's Heart for a time. It was a very practical solution, and it also became an act of solidarity with the staff, the volunteers, and our guests. It opened our eyes to the weight of helping families overcome homelessness. It is one thing to experience the organization from the outside in. Now we were right in the middle of it. We gained a new appreciation for their needs and complexities, which helped me better articulate what we needed to accomplish.

On the first night we moved into the building for our

temporary stay, it was late. We were both tired and ready to crash. We blew up the air mattresses. This is what we were going to sleep on that night. Because I knew it wasn't going to be even close to the mattress we were used to sleeping on, we stacked them on top of one another to make it as comfortable as possible. We finally got into bed and were exhausted. About two hours into the night we woke up to the air mattress caving in on us because the air was leaking out. I was mad and frustrated. That night I woke up four different times to fill each air mattress.

The next day we finished moving and then headed to the store to buy a new air mattress. I refused to have another night like the night before. This time I bought the cream-of-the-crop air mattress in a brand-new box from the store to make it as comfortable as possible. I mean it was the Cadillac of air mattresses.

I finished up a few last-minute moving errands and went back to Sophia's Heart. When I returned, Leyicet had started blowing up the new air mattress. I noticed it was really dirty and looked used. It also had a patch on the underside. It dawned on me that someone had returned a used air mattress in a brand-new box and kept the new one. I wanted to take it back immediately, but Leyicet was exhausted, so we threw a blanket over it and went to sleep.

Only an hour after falling asleep, we woke up yet again to the air mattress sinking. Leyicet wanted to blow it back up and return it in the morning, but I insisted we get up, drive to the store, and return it right then. At that point, I was even more determined and frustrated. So we set out for the store, which was open twenty-four hours. By this time, it was two or three in the morning. I was blurry-eyed and apparently drove through a stop sign.

The magical blue lights pulsated behind our car. As soon as I saw the lights, it dawned on me that this is what it must feel like to the families that stay at Sophia's Heart. One thing after another comes at them until they are frustrated and feel defeated.

Leyicet and I grabbed hands and prayed a small prayer asking

God to help us bear the burdens these homeless and struggling families must feel. We also vowed at that moment to do whatever it takes to make their stay at Sophia's Heart as comfortable and beneficial as possible.

It's a funny story looking back, but in the moment, it really opened my eyes to what our residents go through. It gave me perspective.

That is certainly a strange way to spend eight weeks of your first year of marriage, but I have to give it up to Leyicet. She never complained. If anything, I was the one who found myself complaining. It made me even more resolved to make sure our facility was not just a warm, dry place for families. I wanted our facility to be a place they could be proud of and a place we could call home.

Even today, Leyicet continues to join me for family night every Tuesday when I am in town. It means so much to me that we can share a passion for the same things in life. It begins with two hearts that are attuned with one another and see life through similar eyes. I am constantly impressed by Leyicet's character, which allows her to be fully involved as a volunteer at Sophia's Heart. She is not caught in Sophia's shadow. Leyicet embraces her calling there and carries herself like the loving servant she is. She has brought me so much joy. And the best is yet to come.

Two Become Three

I had secretly hoped the little guy would come on January 8. It was a few weeks before the baby was expected to come, but for me eight is a lucky number of sorts. Many special events in my life are connected to the number eight. My appearance on *American Idol* was on its eighth season, and my first tryout was on 8-8-2008.

However, that didn't happen. The anticipation was eating away at us. When you first learn you are going to have a baby, there is a great deal of excitement about what is ahead. If your wife has a relatively normal pregnancy, as Leyicet did, then you enjoy the time of preparation. But then there comes a time when you are ready for the baby to arrive.

That's where we were the entire month of January 2013. We were already past the middle of the month. Our anticipation had almost turned into frustration. We kept wondering when the baby was going to get here.

Not thinking anything about it, we went to a charity event the night before the baby was due. Leyicet and I were having great time, when she thought she was starting to have contractions. If you've ever been through this before, you know about Braxton Hicks contractions. They aren't real, but you think they are real. The doctor explained it was nature's way of preparing the body for labor and delivery.

It wasn't long before the real thing started. We went to the hospital (but not before stopping by McDonald's). It was early in the morning. It wasn't the best food choice I could have made, but I knew this was likely going to take a while. I had to eat something. I was hungry, and we didn't even have to get out of the car.

Leyicet was in labor most of the day and into the evening. Then the moment we had all been waiting for was finally about to happen. It seemed like seconds, and then we heard the cry of Baby Danny for the first time. It was the most unbelievable experience.

Daniel Emanuel Gokey was born on January 20, 2013, at 8:52 p.m. (CST). He weighed eight pounds and eleven ounces. He had ten fingers and ten toes. He was the most beautiful child I had ever seen.

Time stopped. It felt as if we were floating through another dimension. Nothing mattered but my baby boy.

I couldn't wait to hold him, feed him, and just love him. I knew I would likely have to change diapers, listen to him cry, and set aside my normal sleeping habits, but I tried not to think about those things too much. For me, I couldn't believe this dream had finally come true. I had every reason to believe this would never happen, yet it did.

That day, Leyicet and I became more than just a couple in love with each other. Our family of two has now become a family of three. It is no longer just about our needs, wants, and desires. We no longer have the ability to go to sleep when we are tired, eat when we are hungry, and go wherever and do whatever we feel like in the moment. We are now responsible for the newest member of our family: Baby Danny.

This is a new beginning for both of us. We've never been down this path before. We are absolutely certain we have no idea what we just got ourselves into, but it hasn't kept us from enjoying every little smile, every little movement, every little thing about this guy.

It's also a new beginning for Baby Danny. All he has known up to this point is what it's like to be inside the belly of Leyicet. Now he gets to discover a whole new world. And we're going to be there with him every step of the way.

On that special day, I realized a dream I've had for most of my life: to be a father and have a family of my own.

The Guessing Game

It is an overwhelming responsibility to become a parent, especially with your first one. You're never really quite sure if what your baby is doing is what he is supposed to be doing and if what you're doing is what you're supposed to be doing. It's the ongoing, never-ending guessing game called parenthood. I suspect it will be that way until he can learn to tell us what he feels.

I feel helpless at times. I want to satisfy his every need so he doesn't cry, but I don't know he is in need until he cries. I want to feed him when he is hungry, but I can't tell sometimes if his cry is because he is hungry or needs a new diaper or if he just wants to belt it out for a few minutes.

Baby Danny is so delicate. I want to wrap my arms around him and make sure he never experiences pain, never experiences regret, and never experiences loss. I know he will one day, but I want to do everything within my power to prevent, or at least delay, those experiences in his life.

One day I am going to teach my son the things dads teach their sons. Unfortunately, I'm not much of a mechanic or ballplayer. I can teach him enough of both to be dangerous.

Of course I am going to teach him about music and singing. But I also want to teach him what I've learned about life: things like loving the people around you because you never know how much time you'll have to do that, things like believing in yourself and your dreams even if everyone else tells you they are crazy, things like pushing forward toward realizing your dreams even if you don't feel like it sometimes. I'm going to use my words to encourage him, just like my dad did with me.

I want Baby Danny to live life with the eyes of his heart and the arms of his faith wide open so he can embrace the hope that is before him. There is a reason he is alive. It will be years before he discovers that for himself, but I want to be right there when he does.

There is something exciting and fulfilling to watch a dream you've had be shattered and then brought back to life. When Sophia died, I thought it was all over. I didn't think I had the strength to love again. I didn't know if I would ever be a dad, yet here I am holding Baby Danny in my arms. Thrilled doesn't begin to describe what I am feeling inside.

More to Come

The ancients believed that the birth of a child was a signal that new things were about to happen. Baby Danny is a reminder that my destiny is not complete. In fact, I have yet to fully uncover all that is ahead of me. I believe that is just as true for you as it is for me.

I believe your best days are ahead of you.

I believe abundance is coming your way.

I believe fulfillment is within your reach.

I believe your new beginning starts today.

I believe because I know that hope is right in front of you. You will be able to see it too if you are bold enough to open the eyes of your heart and the arms of your faith.

There is so much more to come. Don't give up too soon.

Whatever it is that you are going through, I want you to know it won't last forever.

Whatever it is that is heavy on your heart, I want you to know that the pain will go away.

Whatever it is that is troubling you, I want you to know that better days are ahead.

Had I given up, I never would have found Leyicet and been able to love again. I might never have become a father.

There is no amount of success, money, power, or position that can replace love. It is the foundation of our hope and the strength in our resolve to continue to move toward our purpose in life. When you believe, you will find the strength to exchange anxiety for faith, regret for new beginnings, and addiction for victory. Your life is not finished. Love is not impossible. You have yet to accomplish all you were designed to accomplish. Something better is always ahead of you. Even in the darkest moments, new life is being created and spoken into reality through your faith and trust that hope remains always in front of you.

Chapter 17

Hope in Front of You

Faith spins not by what you see but by what you believe.

If you get nothing else from my story, I want you to remember that whatever obstacles you face, whatever roadblocks you encounter, whatever failures you experience, it's not the end of the road. Rather, it is life's way of preparing you and conditioning you for what's still to come. I would not be who I am had I not gone through everything I've been through. The same is true for you, too. It's part of what makes you unique and set apart to accomplish your divine destiny.

You have been created for something special. You have a purpose. You were not placed on this earth to just go through the motions. Our time on earth is too short to not find significance, purpose, and meaning through how we live and the things in which we choose to invest.

You have been gifted in a unique way. That doesn't mean you're going to become a celebrity, well known, popular, or famous. None of that stuff matters because it doesn't last anyway. What matters is that we live out the story God has written for our lives and also do something with the opportunities we've been given to impact the lives of the people around us. All we have to do is say yes to the needs around us. They are many, and they are great. You have the capacity to respond.

You have been positioned to make a difference. You have been placed where you are for a reason. It doesn't mean you're going to stay there. It doesn't mean it is forever. It doesn't mean you can't rise above it. But right now you are where you are. Start there. Look around. Discover how you can be you and help others experience abundance and blessing.

You have been empowered to act. The time to put the words we speak into motion is now. Change is not created by sitting around and waiting for the perfect opportunity. Change happens when we make a decision to act. If I hadn't decided to get out of debt, I would still be there. If I hadn't married Sophia, I would have missed God's gift to me through her living—and her dying. If I hadn't tried out for *American Idol,* I would have missed an opportunity to influence others for good. If I hadn't started Sophia's Heart, families would be on the street with no safe place to stay.

You have everything you need to take the next step. That's right. Don't wait until you have more money, more time, or more of whatever you think you need. You have all you need to take the next step right now.

The Challenge

It is an interesting notion to consider that life would come without challenges, yet we are surprised when the challenges come. We spend the first years of our lives overcoming impossible things. During that time, we learn how to walk, talk, and eat solid food. We don't know enough to complain about how impossible those tasks are when we begin life, so we try, try, and try again until we are able to do them.

My challenge to you is to let go of your preconceived ideas about life. The idea that life should be anything less than a series of obstacles and overcoming those obstacles. The greater our elevation in life, the bigger the obstacles. Our goal should be to gain confidence and perspective along the way that gives us courage and perseverance through those difficult moments.

We cross a line when we think we deserve something. That doesn't mean we can't anticipate good things; it simply means we shouldn't expect the details to always work themselves out. Life is a verb, just like love. Until we put what we believe into motion, it won't reshape the world around us.

Faith Matters

There is a reason why the words *faith* and *hope* are often used together. They both describe the same thing. It takes faith to practice hope, and to practice hope without faith is impossible. We must believe we are playing out a divine destiny in our lives. Without that, there is nothing pulling us forward through the successes and failures that will absolutely come.

It's easy to believe that bad stuff will come. Maybe life has beat you up. Maybe you feel used up, counted out, and finished. But even though it's harder to believe the good stuff than the bad, faith tells me you are not any of those things.

My heart was ripped out of my chest when Sophia died. I didn't want to do anything. I was numb, broken, and beat up. I just wanted to quit. But I didn't stay there. I forced myself to let go of the pain and allowed myself to believe again.

You may have been through some dark moments. You may have so much pain in your life right now that you can't see straight. You may be wondering if life is even worth living. I want to be absolutely clear: Your life is worth living because you matter. You may have to tell yourself that thousands of times before you start to feel it in your gut. But don't give up and give in.

Grab on to What Is True

Faith points us to what is true. For something to be true, it has to be completely true. If there is one truth, then it applies to all people in all places and times. What's important about that is this: Truth is available to everyone. It doesn't require a special knowledge, a certain level of income, or even a certain position. Truth is a gift we discover as we believe in hope and act on faith.

I find the greatest amount of truth when I am serving another person. It could be my wife, my son, or someone I don't even know. Relationships are heaven's way of reminding us what life was meant to be about in the first place: people.

When we serve other people, we recognize that we possess the power to impact the life of someone else in a positive way. If we can impact others in a positive way, we can also impact our lives in a positive way. But we must let go of our illusions so we can be free to grab on to what is true.

I find the least amount of truth when I am so focused on myself that I don't see the needs of other people. If your heart is hard, your attitude indifferent, and your posture exclusive, you are likely missing your meaning and purpose in life. It isn't contained in the obvious things but rather in the form of personal relationships.

Some of those relationships will be temporary. Some will last forever. Some will simply be in passing. It doesn't matter. When our hearts are open to what is ahead, we connect with those around us and remember that purpose and meaning are hidden treasures found within the people we choose to love.

The key to maintaining good relationships is to keep a short memory and forgive quickly, because forgiveness is always the answer. Holding on to offenses will only keep you bound. Anger only hurts you, not the person you are angry at, whether you feel justified or not. Forgiveness is freedom.

Hope Is Real

You might be bitter. You might be spent emotionally, physically, and spiritually. I don't know what you've been through, but I know what I've been through, and I can say with conviction that what pulled me through my darkest moments was the thread of hope I followed. Without that, I don't think I would be where I am today. In fact, I know I wouldn't.

Hope connects us to the eternal life source and becomes a lifeline when tragedy strikes. Hope is what reminds us that life exists beyond what we can see, taste, touch, and feel.

When you change the words you use to describe your life, you suddenly discover that what seemed like a dead end was really a detour, what felt like a destination was really a delay, and what appeared to be a sign of distress was really an opportunity to discover something new. Hope is always in front of you, but it requires that you look at life through the eyes of your heart. The challenge is to daily protect your heart and not allow deadly emotions to blind you from seeing hope.

The Unseen

I believe in unseen things. In a way, you could say I always have. But when you've watched people you love dance between the lines of life and death, when you've lived on the stage of the world, when you've experienced the setbacks and the victories I have, you have no choice but to conclude that something greater than this world can contain exists.

You can feel the strength that comes from the most unlikely places and in the most unexpected ways. It is confirmed in our drive to continue in the midst of impossible odds, in our will to stand when it is easy to fall, in our endurance when it would just be easier to give up. Just because something is unseen doesn't mean it is uncertain, impossible, or foolish.

Hope is unseen—that is, until you start looking for it. Then you find it in the face of a little child whose stomach is now full, the smile of a father who knows his family is safe and warm, and the strength of an individual to finally kick an addiction that has been kicking him for years.

Some question whether God exists. I don't. I see Him everywhere. And I see Him most often among the poor, hungry, homeless, and hopeless. We are closest to God when we are with people in need. Why? Because they remind us that we are in need of faith, hope, and love too.

I Believe

Belief is a tricky thing. We want to possess it because we think we can control it. But belief in things we can control really isn't belief at all. Instead, we must believe in what we have yet to experience because that is what is required to find hope.

I believe your best days are ahead of you. You have likely been through a lot. I have too. If you've lived any length of time on this earth, you have experienced difficulty and disappointment. Hope reminds us the best is yet to come.

I believe you have yet to discover the depths of your giftedness. Every obstacle we overcome teaches us about life and about ourselves. You are living in the midst of your destiny right now and may not even realize it. It may be years before you are able to connect the dots. But hope points us forward.

I believe you have good things in your future. No matter how high you've been or how low you've gone, there are good things in your future. You were created to do great things. And starting that journey begins right where you are today. You won't fully understand the direction you're headed, but you can be certain that today is laying the groundwork for something special.

I believe your destiny is greater than what you can dream today.

Every step of the way will feel new. I couldn't have predicted or imagined the different twists and turns that my life would take. But I did have a sense that what was coming was greater than where I was and where I had been. If I had never let go of the pain in my past, I couldn't have reached forward to what was coming.

I believe you have a divine purpose. Your life is full of meaning and purpose. That doesn't mean bad things won't happen. I can assure you they will. But when you remember that your life is a constant unfolding of your divine destiny, you begin to pay attention to what you can see — and what you can't. It's not this world where we will fully understand how all the pieces fit together; it's in the world to come. In the meantime, hope assures us that we do have purpose and significance this side of heaven.

Let Go Before You Leap

I remember watching kids swing across the monkey bars on the playground at school. It was an art for some. They moved so swiftly you would think they were walking on air. In order to move from one bar to the next, you have to let go of the bar you are holding on to in order to grab the next one. If you don't, you will lose momentum and stop moving forward.

When the dark moments come — and they will come — the temptation is to not let go of the pain, hurt, and suffering. Instead, you may choose to dwell on it. But you can't let yourself stay there.

I didn't want to let Sophia go. She was the love of my life. Why did she have to die so soon? I was stuck on that question long enough for it to become toxic. My anger was so poisonous that it was far worse than the tragedy that sparked it. I lost my way and lost touch with my divine destiny. I was so stuck in the middle of my tragedy that I couldn't see the good things happening right in front of me. I had made it on *American Idol.* This was the dream Sophia and I shared, and it was coming true. Yet it took some time to see that because of my poisoned heart.

What are you holding on to that is becoming toxic in your life? It's okay to feel pain inside. It is what makes you human. It's not okay to allow that pain and suffering to govern you and cloud your vision of the good things that are before you. You have to let go, just like I did.

Maybe you are in the midst of addiction; let go and leap.

Maybe you are in the midst of failure; let go and leap.

Maybe you are in the midst of stress; let go and leap.

Maybe you are hanging on to toxic emotions from situations you can't control; let go and leap.

Whatever it is that has a grip on you, let go and leap.

You are special, and you were designed to accomplish something you've been uniquely gifted to do. Your divine destiny is before you. All you have to do is leap. So leap into the hope that is before you. It's the only way you'll find your life's purpose, even in the midst of your darkest moments.

Conclusion

Life is not religious. It is not political. It is not black. It is not white. It is neither rich nor poor, powerful nor weak, intelligent nor ignorant. Life is only this: love.

Part of recognizing that we must live in harmony with our divine destiny is acknowledging that it is not discovered in meditation and contemplation alone. Rather, our discovery comes in the doing. It comes when we roll up our sleeves and hang ourselves out there, even when the possibility of failure is great.

I had to face this reality during two significant events in my life that happened almost simultaneously. One was the death of my first wife, Sophia. The second was my time on *American Idol.* The act of letting go of Sophia was just that: action. I thought about letting go a hundred times, but I kept hanging on. It wasn't until I decided to act on it that something changed.

The second time I had to take a step that was overwhelmingly scary to me was choosing to audition for *American Idol.* If I'd never showed up in Kansas City, I would have guaranteed my failure and the end of any hope at a music career. (It's possible another path would have opened, but it was very unlikely.)

Each week I had to step on that stage and sing my heart out. It was terrifying to realize that millions of people were critiquing my every move. Then I had to stand there and let industry professionals tell me what was great and not so great about my performance. Yet every week I forced myself to find the courage to do it all over again.

Sophia's Heart came about because I took a step of faith in a direction that was unpredictable. I had never started or run a nonprofit before. Sure, I had been on the staff of a nonprofit, but leading one was entirely different. We have faced and will continue to face insurmountable odds. But in the midst of every reason to give up and retreat, we are making the difference in the lives of people who have no other choice or option.

Discover Hidden Treasure

Some people think the greatest treasure is found in balance sheets and bank accounts. I disagree. I know a lot of unhappy rich people who are alone, confused, and out of touch with their divine purpose and who they are designed to be. The greatest treasure is found in the most unlikely places: within the hearts of people.

I know that sounds like a cliché and is overused. The problem with clichés is that we've heard them so much that we stop thinking about them critically. Life is about relationships with people, not things you can own or possess. The happiest people in the world are those who have deep connections with other people. And sometimes that's all they have.

People sometimes look at others as a burden or a line item on a budget sheet. Not true. People are a gift. I don't mean just the pretty people, the perfect people, the holy people, or the special people. I mean *all* people, especially those who aren't pretty, perfect, holy, or special.

Step into Your Destiny

I didn't want you to read this book so you could find a way to pass the time. I want to inspire you not to allow the unpredictable, unfortunate, and unexplainable to keep you from living into all you were created to be and accomplish. But that means when we find healing within ourselves, we then have a responsibility to help heal others.

The richest people in the world are the ordinary people who generously give their time, unique giftedness, and resources to invest in others. Therein lies the accumulated potential of each soul, sometimes realized, sometimes wasted. In each one of us is planted all the potential to be everything God created us to be.

No matter where you live, what level of education you have, or how perfect your life appears, there is part of you that needs to be healed, mended, and put back together. No house, car, or job can ever complete you. You will always be left unsatisfied. That's because you were created to find your completeness in sharing and helping others.

Prepare for the Unexpected

Some people don't take action because they don't feel prepared, qualified, or ready to act. Here is a hint: No one does. Do you think I was fully prepared at every turn to take the next step? Do you think I didn't have to overcome the fear that comes with doing something new? Do you think I've never made a mistake? (If you do, I recommend you flip to the front of the book and start reading there.) I've made a bunch of mistakes. But it was in my doing that I discovered the various connection points that led me to where I am today.

You might never start a nonprofit, experience the loss of a loved one, or audition for a TV show. So what? You have been placed, platformed, and prepared to start making a difference right where you are. Just say yes to the opportunities as they come your way.

You must hold loosely to the things in this world so you have the ability to grab hold of what will last forever. When we are attached to one way of doing things or only one way of understanding the world around us, our minds limit our opportunities. When we open our minds to new things, we begin to see unlimited people and opportunities within arm's reach.

Identify Something to Live For

Sophia's Heart gave me something to live for. If I didn't have purpose, I may not have survived the deep depression I experienced after my loss. If I didn't have someone to serve, I may never have found the healing that made me whole again. If I didn't have a dream of the future, I might not have had the energy to continue to push through the obstacles and reach through the unknown to fully live into my purpose, mission, and destiny.

You can't wait around for "the right moment" because the right moment will never come. People who wait around for some big epiphany rarely experience it. They risk wasting their lives and miss the blessing that comes from showing love to other people, especially those in need. On the other hand, people who practice love as a verb and put their lives into action discover that the epiphany always comes in the doing.

Every successful person I've met understands the need to have something to live for that is bigger than just the day-to-day details. Those who have this perspective see it as a thread that pulls them through the times when the feelings aren't there, the breaks don't come, and the stakes seem too high.

If we don't have something to live for and someone to serve, we risk being caught up in building our own kingdoms instead of helping others live into their divine destinies. If we make life all about us, our world becomes very small. If we make life about people and relationships, we discover a wealth that is limitless and has the power to create a positive change.

Find a way to put your convictions into action. Again, change doesn't happen by sitting around and dreaming. There is a time for that. But right now, the best way to find hope is to stare it square in the face and move toward it by helping others discover it for the very first time.

Find a Community

Find a community of people who can help you thrive. When I say community, I don't mean social media. That is a great tool to help foster an existing community of people, but it is not a substitute for the real thing. Look for a group of people who care about the things you do, and find a way to get involved.

When I first discovered my interest in business and being an entrepreneur, I started hanging around people who were successful in business. I wanted to pick their brains. I asked them questions, and they challenged me to take steps toward my dream. It was a very healthy process.

Don't join just any community. Look for people who share a similar perspective of the world, are passionate about the same things you are, and desire to put their convictions into action. Also, look for people who see things in you that you didn't see in yourself. I've had a number of people speak things into my life and recognize things in me that I didn't know were there before.

I think it's easy to become really busy or substitute any number of things for investing in the lives of people. Technology is great. I use it every day, but Leyicet and I aren't going to raise our son through a computer screen. It's through laughing together, crying together, and doing life together that we will be able to teach him the things we have learned along the way.

In the same way, look for people who you know are ethical and moral and genuinely care for others. If you're wondering if the people you spend your time with are the right community of friends and mentors, ask yourself this question: Does being around them bring out the best or the worst in me? If your answer is anything but that they cause the best to come out in you, you need to find a new community of people.

Give Yourself Away

There is a principle I learned early in my twenties when I discovered generosity. I can't give away so much that I will go broke. In fact, the opposite is true. The less I give away, the less chance that what I have will be multiplied.

I have found time and time again that when I give more than I think I should, the miracle happens. It comes back to me many times over. Your purpose—your divine calling—includes living a generous life.

That means giving away your time. Nonprofits in your community are desperately looking for volunteers. Pick something you're passionate about and get involved. Give your time, look the people in need right in the face, and you'll discover what really matters in this life and the life to come.

That means giving away your skills. You have been uniquely gifted and empowered with some skill. It could be as simple as a warm smile or the ability to make a great meal, or it could be as complex as starting a nonprofit or fighting for some change in public policy. Don't spend all your talent on the things you think will secure power, position, and prestige. Remember, fame comes and goes. Your legacy will live forever in the hearts and minds of the people you've helped and served.

That means giving away your money. I have spent most of my life without what I would consider an abundance of money. It was when I was in over my head with debt that I decided to start being generous. It didn't make sense, it didn't add up, but something deep within moved me to start being generous in whatever way I could. For me, that's when my life really started to come together and things started to change.

Don't believe the lie that you don't have money to give. Generosity is a choice. You have money to give to support the people in your community trying to help others in need. You'll discover the multiplying effect generosity will have on your spirit, family, and wallet.

Dare to Dream

One of the activities every person who comes through Sophia's Heart participates in is an exercise where we help them identify a more desirable future that is specific to them. When we change our minds, we change the altitude at which we can live. When we change our direction, we change the momentum at which we can move. When we change our dreams, we ultimately change the destination where we will arrive.

You were meant for more. Even better, you are the key to someone else unlocking their divine destiny. But if you can't see that, you'll miss the blessing. It all begins when you dare to dream about what is in front of you rather than hanging on to what is behind you.

When you dream, a new energy emerges.

Your stumble is transformed into a steady pace.

Your doubt is transformed into an assurance of what has yet to be seen.

Your lack of abundance is transformed into an overabundance.

You suddenly have the strength to stand.

You suddenly have the freedom to dream.

You suddenly have the clarity to move forward.

Hope is not behind you.

Hope is not beside you.

Hope is in front of you, and it is asking you to dream, believe, and unleash your divine purpose so you can serve the world as you reach toward that which will last forever.

This is your hope. And it is right in front of you.

Scan to hear a personal message from Danny on hope.

About the Author

BMG recording artist DANNY GOKEY became a favorite of millions of fans as a top-three finalist on season 8 of *American Idol.* In 2010, Gokey released his debut album, *My Best Days*, which garnered record first-week retail and digital album sales for a male debut artist in his musical genre and peaked at number four on the weekly Billboard 200 album chart. He is the founder of Sophia's Heart, a nonprofit organization established in 2008 in honor of his late wife. The organization's goal is to give hope and housing to homeless families as well as provide scholarships to deserving students and operate a thriving inner-city music and arts program.

Connect with Danny Gokey

www.dannygokey.com

www.facebook.com/DannyGokeyOfficial

www.twitter.com/DannyGokey (@DannyGokey)

http://www.youtube.com/DannyGokey

About Sophia's Heart

In 2008, Sophia's Heart was founded by Danny Gokey to help children and families who have been touched by poverty, sickness, broken homes, and broken dreams. The organization provides transitional housing for homeless families while seeking to rebuild confidence and the motivation to dream again. The program accomplishes these goals by providing coaching in the areas of life skills, job training, financial planning, spiritual inspiration, and health and wellness. Sophia's Heart also serves to inspire creativity in children through a thriving music and performing arts education program that allows inner-city kids to express themselves and pursue their dreams in a safe, supportive environment. To find out more about Sophia's Heart, go to Sophiasheart.org.